moreJESUS

more JESUS

Michael DeFazio

Published by Real Life Church
23841 Newhall Ranch Road
Valencia, CA 91355
www.reallifechurch.org

Published in association with Samizdat Creative
www.samizdatcreative.com

ISBN 978-1-938633-04-1

Cover design by Joshua Heyer
www.heyerdesign.com

To Connie DeFazio

Thanks for making me memorize chapter three.

Contents

Acknowledgements

Paul spills more ink encouraging thankfulness in Colossians than any other letter, largely because he knows we're better protected from lies when we're thinking about how much God has done for us. Studying Colossians has overwhelmed me with gratitude for how God has saved us in Christ and how deeply he desires to grow us up in him. Writing on Colossians has overwhelmed me with gratitude for the people I get to grow up with.

If I tried to think of all the people who have helped me understand the Bible in general, more specifically the Apostle Paul, and even more specifically the book of Colossians, I'd never finish. So I'll stick to those who helped with this particular project.

Thanks to Dotty, Bob, and DaAnne Smith for lending me a place to study Colossians. Little did I know at the time it would lead to this. Thanks to Rusty George for giving me the green light to write. Thanks to Real Life Church as a whole for being such a wonderful community to write for. Thanks to Jason VanderPal, Rob Baldwin, Marilyn Lombardi, and Steve Whitney for picking up the slack while I've been preoccupied. Thanks to Fred Gray for forcing me to mind my audience. Thanks to Amy Storms for assisting with the research. Without your help I'd be very boring. Thanks to Mark Moore and Chris Dewelt for the tour of Paul's actual journeys, and to Dan Hamel for helpful conversations along the way. Speaking of helpful conversations, thanks to Jim Johnson for reminding me to clarify the gospel and stick to the text.

Thanks to Michelle Gabriele, Jeff Figearo, Alex Megarit, and Chip Bologitz for your feedback. Chip, you could get paid for this. Big thanks to Caleb Seeling, Mike DeVries, and especially Kate Holburn at Samizdat Creative. Once again it has been a joy to work with your team. And biggest thanks of all, of course, to my Beth. You didn't just improve this book. You give me reason to believe and live what I've written.

Special thanks also to my mother Connie DeFazio, to whom the book is dedicated. When I was a teenager you told me to memorize Colossians 3, explaining that if I learned and lived only this I would have a pretty solid grasp on what it means to live Christianly. And to answer your questions, this is what I stand for; this is who I represent. Thanks in large part to you.

Introduction

I love Italian food. All of it. Bruschetta. Focaccia. Gnocchi. Pasta. Meatballs. Sauce. Linguini. Ravioli. Tortellini. Fettuccini Alfredo. Manicotti Formaggio. Spaghetti a la Carbonara. Lasagna. Pizza. And yes, Cannoli. I don't discriminate between restaurants either. I'd just as soon eat at Fazoli's as Olive Garden, Maggiano's, or the place you love that I've never heard of.

So you can imagine how eager I was when, just a few months ago, I had the opportunity to travel to Rome for the first time in my life. Of course I was excited about the history and tracing Paul's final steps and all those wonderful things. But I was also thrilled about the food.

It was . . . okay.

Don't get me wrong, I'd go again in a heartbeat and enthusiastically eat whatever you put in front of me. And the coffee? Best in the world, hands down. But suffice it to say, neither my mind nor my palette were blown by the cuisine.

So let me start over. I love American Italian food. I love Cali-Itali. This is neither strange nor scandalous. Many of us "love Mexican food" even if we've never eaten it. Our Mex is Tex and our Chinese is American, as is our Thai and sushi. Mixing foods from different cultures often leads to full tummies and happy taste buds.

But mixing doesn't work for everything.

Imagine if you went to dinner one Tuesday evening at our local Italian restaurant, and when you arrived you ran into me dining with a woman who is not my wife. You might find this a bit odd, maybe even call me on it. And what would you think if I offered the following explanation?

"Back off, friend, today is Tuesday. Date night with Beth is Thursday, and you can rest assured that 48 hours from now, she and I will be sitting right here at this table, renewing our vows and gazing longingly into each other's eyes. But tonight belongs to this woman right here."

So, um, yeah, that doesn't exactly work. Some things mix. Others don't.[1]

I'm going to say something that I'll bet has never been said before: Jesus is more like a wife than a plate of spaghetti.

Jesus does not mix well with others.

You are reading a book based on Paul's letter to first century Christians in Colossae. Colossae was an interesting city in the ancient Roman Empire. On the one hand, it was tiny and insignificant – the least important of all the cities Paul wrote to. On the other hand, its location along a recent trade route had exposed Colossian culture to a wide variety of outside influences – political, religious, and otherwise.

Into this mix came the gospel of Jesus Christ. Unlike so many places Paul served, he wasn't the one who first brought the gospel to Colossae. Matter of fact, as far as we know he never even visited. But during his years leading churches in the nearby city of Ephesus, Paul met a native Colossian named Epaphras. Epaphras listened to Paul and realized he'd found something unique and beautiful and true, so he became a follower of this Messiah named Jesus. Some time later, Epaphras took the message of Jesus back to Colossae and planted a few churches. Meanwhile he became an important part of Paul's team.

A few years down the road, Epaphras and Paul became aware of problems among the Jesus-followers in Colossae. To put it simply, they were mixing Jesus with other religious elements – mostly from ancient Judaism with a pinch of folk spirituality and a dash of Roman propaganda thrown in. As was his custom, Paul wrote a letter in response.

He didn't know these people personally, so he couldn't just scold and scream like he did with the Galatians. As a result the world received one of its most powerful literary and theological treasures – the book of Colossians.

Paul's strategy in Colossians is simple: Give them Jesus. Paul aims to outflank all spiritual, religious, and political competitors by fixing our gaze laser-style on the complete sufficiency of Jesus Christ. Jesus is literally everything we need. Or so Paul would have us believe.

Paul's letter took the Colossians on a particular journey. My goal in *moreJESUS* is to guide you along that same path. I want you to think what

---

[1] I owe this analogy to Kyle Idleman's sermon "Gods at War" (preached 6/24/12 at Southland Christian Church in Lexington, KY). Kyle is one of the teaching pastors at Southeast Christian Church in Louisville, KY.

Paul wanted them to think. To feel what he wanted them to feel. To see what he wanted them to see.

Introductions get boring fast, so let me say a few things about this book and we'll get to it. This is not a commentary. I won't be walking through the text phrase-by-phrase defining every word, explaining every verb tense, and describing all the relevant background information. Commentaries are great, but let's be honest – most of you will never read one. This book is a series of reflections designed, as I said above, to recreate in your heart and mind – and I hope, your life – what this letter's original recipients experienced.

This book is arranged to guide you through Colossians in six weeks. Each section contains a short introduction and seven individual chapters – one for every day of the week. You don't have to treat the chapters as daily readings, of course. My feelings won't be hurt if you devour multiple chapters in one sitting! But the idea is that you can study Colossians 10-15 minutes per day and digest the entire letter in less than two months.

If you want to get the most out of this study, I'd also suggest you read Colossians in its entirety 3-4 times per week. If you can't do this, at the very least be sure to closely read whatever verses each respective chapter aims to unpack. I've provided my own fresh translation for you to read alongside whatever standard version you prefer.

Finally, let me say thanks. I'm glad you've decided to take this journey with us. I hope by the end of it you see what Paul saw, what I am starting to see along with him. I hope you walk away convinced that you don't need more than Christ. All you need is more of what you've already been given. All you need is more Jesus.

Paul's Letter to the Colossians

Paul, an apostle of Christ Jesus by the will of God, together with brother Timothy.

To those set apart in Colossae – the faithful brothers and sisters in Christ. Grace to you and peace from God our Father.

We give thanks to the God and Father of our Lord Jesus Christ in all our prayers for you, having heard of your faith in Christ Jesus and the love you have for all those set apart, a faith and love rooted in the hope that is safely reserved for you in heaven. This you previously heard about in the true message of the gospel, which has come to you just as in all the world it is bearing fruit and growing. It has done the same thing in you from the first day you heard and came to know the truth of God's grace, as you learned it from Epaphras our close friend and co-slave. He is faithful on our behalf as a servant of Christ; he also made clear to us your love in the Spirit.

Because of this, from the first day we heard about you we have not stopped praying for you and asking that you be filled with the knowledge of God's will in all Spiritual wisdom and understanding, so that you may walk in a manner worthy of the Lord that pleases him in every way: bearing fruit in every kind of good work and growing in the knowledge of God, being strengthened with all power according to the might of his glory so you always have endurance and patience, joyfully giving thanks to the Father, who has qualified us to receive a share in the inheritance of those set apart in the light, who delivered us out of the dominion of darkness and transferred us into the kingdom of his beloved Son, in whom we have redemption, the forgiveness of sins.

He is the image of the invisible God,
    firstborn over all creation,
        for in him all things were created –
            in the heavens and on earth,
            things visible and invisible,
            whether thrones or lordships or rulers or authorities.
        All things have been created through him and to him,

    and he is before all things
        and in him all things hold together;
    and he is the head of the body, the church.

He is the founder,
    firstborn from among the dead,
        so that in everything he might enjoy supremacy,

for in him all the Fullness was pleased to permanently dwell,
and through him to reconcile all things to him –
making peace through the blood of his cross –
whether things on earth or things in the heavens.

You too were once alienated, hostile in thought because of your evil deeds, but now he reconciled you in Christ's fleshly body through death, to present you holy and blameless and innocent in his sight, if indeed you continue in the faith, having been solidly established and firmly built, and don't get dislodged from the hope of the gospel you've heard. This gospel has been preached in all creation under heaven, and I, Paul, became its servant.

Now I rejoice in suffering on your behalf, and I fill up in my flesh what is lacking of Christ's afflictions on behalf of his body, which is the church, of which I became a servant according to the commission God gave me: to fill up the word of God for you, the mystery which was hidden from past ages and generations, but now has been made visible to those set apart. To them God chose to make known the richness of the glory of this mystery among the Gentiles, which is Christ in you, the hope of glory. He is the one we publicly proclaim, admonishing everyone and teaching everyone in all wisdom, so that we might present everyone mature in Christ. To this end I labor intensely, striving with all his energy which powerfully energizes me.

I want you to know how intensely I have struggled for you and those in Laodicea – for all those I haven't met in person – that their hearts might be encouraged, having been woven together in love. I want them to come to all fullness of the full assurance of understanding and knowledge of the mystery of God, which is Christ, in whom are hidden all the treasures of wisdom and knowledge. I tell you this so that none of you might be deceived by ideas that sound good on the surface. For I may be absent in flesh, but I am with you in Spirit, rejoicing and seeing your orderliness and the stability of your faith in Christ.

Therefore, just as you received Christ Jesus as Lord, continue walking in him, having been rooted and now being built up in him and being confirmed in the faith just as you were taught, overflowing with thanksgiving. Be on guard so that no one takes you captive through some philosophy, some empty seduction that is based on human tradition, taking its cues from the elemental forces of the world rather than from Christ.

For in him dwells all the fullness of Deity in bodily form, and you are in him where you have already been made complete. He is the head of all rule and authority. And in him you were circumcised with a circumcision not done by human hands, but by stripping off the body of flesh in the circumcision of Christ, having been buried with him in baptism. In him you were also raised, through faith in the working of God who raised him from the dead. And though you were dead in your transgressions and in the uncircumcision of your flesh, he made you alive together with him, having graciously forgiven us all our transgressions, having erased the debt record which was against us with its decrees that opposed us; he has done away with it, having nailed it to the cross. Having disarmed the rulers and authorities, he publicly exposed them, having led them in a Triumphal Procession in him.

Therefore, don't let anyone pass judgment on you regarding food and drink, or because of feasts, new moon celebrations, or sabbaths. All these are a shadow of the things that were to come – the reality is Christ. Let no one rule against you who delights in humility and angelic worship, which he has seen upon entering a visionary trance. He is vainly inflated by the mind of his flesh and isn't holding fast to the head, from whom the whole body – nourished and woven together by its joints and muscles – grows with the growth that comes from God.

If you died with Christ from the elemental forces of the world, why, as though living in the world, do you submit to its regulations? "Do not handle! Do not taste! Do not touch!" All these are destined to perish in their use, and are based on human commands and teachings. Though they have an appearance of wisdom in their self-imposed worship, humility, and harsh treatment of the body, they are completely worthless and serve only to indulge the flesh.

If, therefore, you were raised with Christ, seek the things above, where Christ is, where he is sitting at the right hand of God. Focus on things above, not on earthly things. For you died, and your life has been hidden with Christ in God. Whenever Christ – who is your life – is revealed, then you also will be revealed with him in glory.

Put to death, therefore, the earthly parts: sexual immorality, impurity, impulsiveness, evil desires, and greed which is idolatry. Because of these God's wrath is coming. In them you too used to walk when you were living in these ways, but now also take off all such things as anger, rage, hatred, slander, and abusive words out of your mouth. Don't lie to one another, since you have stripped off the old humanity with its practices and have clothed yourself with the new, which is being renewed in knowledge according to the image of its Creator. Here there is no Greek and Jew, circumcision and uncircumcision, foreigner, savage, slave, or free, but Christ is all and in all.

Clothe yourselves, therefore, as God's chosen people, set apart and loved, with genuine compassion, kindness, humility, gentleness, and patience, bearing with one another and graciously forgiving each other if anyone has a complaint against another. Just as the Lord graciously forgave you, you do the same. And over all these things put on love, which binds them together perfectly. And let the peace of Christ arbitrate in your hearts; into this peace you were called in one body. And be thankful. Let the word

6

of Christ dwell in you richly, teaching and admonishing each other in all wisdom with psalms, hymns, and spiritual songs, singing with gratitude in your hearts to God. And whatever you do, whether in word or deed, do it all in the name of the Lord Jesus, giving thanks to God the Father through him.

Wives, place yourselves under your husbands, as is fitting in the Lord. Husbands, love your wives and do not resent them. Children, obey your parents in all things, for this is pleasing in the Lord. Fathers, don't push your children too hard, so they don't become discouraged. Slaves, in all things obey your earthly masters, not just when they're looking – as if you were just pleasing men – but with a sincere heart, fearing the Lord. Whatever you do, work from the soul, as if for the Lord and not for a human, knowing that from the Lord you will receive the rewarded inheritance. Serve this Lord – Christ – for anyone acting unjustly will receive back injustice for his actions, and there is no partiality. Masters, provide justice and fairness for the slaves, knowing that you also have a Master in heaven.

Continue persistently in prayer, staying alert in it with thanksgiving, and also praying for us so that God might open to us a door for the word, so we can tell the mystery of Christ for which I have been bound, so that I might disclose it appropriately. Walk wisely toward outsiders, capitalizing on the moment. May your speech always be gracious, seasoned with salt so you'll know how you should answer each person.

Tychicus will tell you all about me. He is a beloved brother, faithful servant, and fellow bondslave in the Lord, and I sent him to you for this very reason, that you might know what's going on in my life and that your hearts might be encouraged. I sent him with Onesimus the beloved brother, who is one of your own. They'll tell you everything happening here. Aristarchus my fellow prisoner greets you. Also, if Mark (Barnabas's cousin, about whom you received a command) comes to you then welcome him, and also Jesus who is called Justus. Among my coworkers for the kingdom of God only these are Jewish, and they became a comfort to me.

Epaphras greets you, and he too is one of your own, a servant of Christ Jesus, always striving in the prayers on your behalf, so that you might stand mature and completely full in all God's will. I testify for him that he has great concern for you, as well as those in Laodicea and Hierapolis. Luke the beloved doctor greets you, and Demas too. Greet the brothers and sisters in Laodicea, and Nympha and those in the church that gathers in her house. And whenever you read this letter, see to it that it is also read in the Laodicean church, and you also read the one from Laodicea. And tell Archippus, "See to the ministry which you received in the Lord, that you fulfill it."

I, Paul, write this greeting in my own hand. Remember my chains. Grace be with you.

moreJESUS part 1 – MEMORY

My two-year-old daughter loves watching old videos of herself on my phone. "Old" is, of course, a relative term, because she's two. Her recent favorite is five minutes of her walking around a sand-and-water table while Beth and I coax her to say, "Oh my goodness!" It eventually worked, and it was as adorable as we'd hoped.

There are times as a parent when you wish your kid had the capacity to tell you what's going on in their little brain or heart, and for me her watching herself on camera is one of them.

One time my mom sent me some old videos from when I was a bit older than Claire. I watched with delight until it came to my birthday party where my older sister "helped" by opening all my gifts for me. I was ticked. I probably would have walked to her house immediately if she didn't live 1800 miles away. Instead I confronted her over the phone, and I'm pretty sure she thought (a) I was overreacting and (b) the whole thing was hilarious. "I can't change the fact that you needed my help," she smiled and said like only an older sister can.

Whether joyful or painful, memories root us in our own story. To remember is to relive earlier parts of the narrative that made us who we are today.

When the ancient Israelites finally arrived in the Promised Land, God commanded them to immediately retell their story. According to instructions we find in Deuteronomy 26.1-11, they were to bring a basket of fresh fruit to the priest, declare that they had entered the land God promised, and then recite the following:

> "My father was a wandering Aramean, and he went down into Egypt with a few people and lived there and became a great nation, powerful and numerous. But the Egyptians mistreated us and made us suffer, subjecting us to harsh labor. Then we cried out to the LORD, the God of our ancestors, and the LORD heard our voice and saw our misery, toil and oppression. So the LORD brought us out of Egypt with a mighty hand and an outstretched arm, with great terror and with signs and wonders. He brought us to this place and gave us this land, a land

flowing with milk and honey; and now I bring the firstfruits of the soil that you, LORD, have given me."

Then they offered their fruit basket to the Lord and partied with the Levites and foreigners to celebrate "all the good things" God had given. God knew that if they ever forgot the story of what he had done for them, they were gone.

If that doesn't convince you that God thinks memory matters, maybe the hippocampus will. The hippocampus is a peanut-shaped part of your brain that enables you to remember. What's fascinating is that even though we only need one hippocampus to enjoy a well-functioning memory, we have two. If one stops working it's all good as long as the other one stays strong. God so values memory that he built into our brains a backup memory stick just in case the first one goes kaput.

Sometimes I feel like I'm operating on half a hippocampus. I tend to forget things. A lot. One time when we were first married, Beth called and asked me to put the chicken in the crockpot. "Sure, no problem," I said. Then I hung up the phone and immediately forgot about the whole thing. About an hour later, I remembered that she rang, but it took me twenty minutes to recall why. This is normal for me. Recently I was looking over some old notes and found an abbreviated story of a time I gave the pizza delivery guy the wrong phone number – twice. I recall that occurring and the story being hilarious, but I can't tell it to you now. Why? I can't remember what actually happened.

You may not be this bad, but our culture as a whole marginalizes memory. How many phone numbers have you memorized since you bought your first cell phone?

Memory roots us. Memory matters. We can never be reduced to the things we've done or have been done to us, but neither can we be understood without them.

Paul organizes Colossians the way we'd expect from someone trained in the ancient art of persuasion. Many of Paul's teachers recognized the present power of the past. Reminding people where they come from was a popular method for encouraging people to stay the course.[2] They may have tapped

---

[2] Charles Talbert, *Ephesians and Colossians* (Grand Rapids: Baker Academic, 2007), 175-176.

into a truth deeper than they realized. Remember the hippocampus? It's also the part of our brain that enables navigation. It helps us make our way through space without constantly turning the wrong direction. Recalling where we've been exercises the muscle that gets us where we need to go.

Paul writes Colossians so the church will stop forgetting all that Jesus does and is. The letter centers on a poem that contains some of the profoundest truth ever penned. But he can't start with the poem because his readers aren't yet ready to hear it. They think they see Jesus clearly enough, thanks very much. They're wrong, of course, but you can't just tell people that and expect them to keep listening.

So Paul prepares the church to see Jesus' glory by retelling the church her story. Paul spends the first part of Colossians exercising the church's memory muscle. This is who you were and are, what you became part of, what and why you came to believe.

The Colossians are starting to think they've tapped all Jesus had to offer, and that it's time to turn elsewhere for more. Paul gives them (and us) more, but the right kind of more – more of what God has already given. Which raises the question Paul unpacks here at the beginning: What *has* God already done through, in, and on behalf of those he calls his own?

Different
Chapter 1 – Colossians 1.1-2

Do you know who you are?

For better or worse, I am Michael DeFazio. I'm a tall, skinny white guy with brown hair, blue eyes, and one white eyebrow. I love basketball and frisbees and coffee and books. I am a son and a brother from a large Italian family. I am a husband and a father. I am a follower of Jesus.

You are . . . well, I don't know who you are. Do you?

Some would say that how we perceive ourselves governs everything we think, say, and do.

If you consider yourself dumb or uneducated, you won't often offer your opinion in public. If you think you are an athlete or someone who takes care of your body, you're more likely to go to the gym. If you fancy yourself an entrepreneur or risk-taker, you're more likely to try new things. If you think you've got rhythm, you'll probably join a dance ensemble before me.

Does anything motivate more thoroughly than identity? Who we think we are largely determines who we will become. So who are you?

I recently read a news story about a Dallas woman who got in her car one morning, headed to work, and ten hours later found herself 600 miles away in Santa Fe, New Mexico. Confused and exhausted, she checked herself into a hotel room, only to wake up the next morning with no idea where she was, how she got there, or whose face she was looking at in the

13

mirror. When asked what she remembered last, she said, "Nothing." When asked what was going through her mind at the time, she answered, "Fear. A lot of fear."[3]

The world is a scary place, especially when you don't know who you are.

Can you imagine having no idea who you are?

Something about this experience must resonate with us, because we can't stop making and watching movies about forgetting and/or re-discovering who we are. Some are literal amnesia stories, like the Bourne trilogy, *The Notebook, Eternal Sunshine of the Spotless Mind,* or *Spellbound.* Others spin amnesia metaphorically, like *Batman Begins, City Slickers,* or *The Lion King.*

Paul begins Colossians by defining us. By establishing our core identity:

Paul, an apostle of Christ Jesus by the will of God, together with brother Timothy. To those set apart in Colossae – the faithful brothers and sisters in Christ. Grace to you and peace from God our Father.

Ancient letters typically followed a simple pattern: identify sender, identify readers, offer a quick greeting, and get to business. You'll recognize this in almost all of Paul's letters. But don't read too fast, because Paul platforms this convention to make a point.

Here in Colossians 1.1-2 he teaches us who we are.

Those set apart translates the word "holy ones." Holy essentially means "set apart for a special or unique purpose." Think about toothbrushes, for instance. You might use old toothbrushes to clean the toilet or the A/C vents in your car, but you only use the new toothbrush for one task: to brush your teeth. It is set apart. It is holy. Same thing might be true of your favorite pair of earrings or your finest suit.

Not everything is used for anything. Some things are different. *We* are different.

To grasp what Paul means by "holy," we'll need more than a dictionary though. For Paul (and for us) the word is rooted in the story of God calling one nation to be his chosen vessel for reaching the world. After liberating Israel from slavery in Egypt, here is what God said to Moses in Exodus 19:

---

[3] For details, see http://www.cbsnews.com/2100-3445_162-4987604.html. Accessed 5/1/12.

"This is what you are to say to the descendants of Jacob and what you are to tell the people of Israel: 'You yourselves have seen what I did to Egypt, and how I carried you on eagles' wings and brought you to myself. Now if you obey me fully and keep my covenant, then out of all nations you will be my treasured possession. Although the whole earth is mine, you will be for me a kingdom of priests and a holy nation.'"

Did you catch that? God intended this group of ragamuffin ex-slaves to become "a kingdom of priests and a holy nation." Right on the heels of this declaration comes the Ten Commandments, followed by dozens of additional guidelines. Many laws taught them how to live *differently* than the surrounding nations. Everyone else may serve human kings, but *you* are to serve God alone. Everyone else may oppress the poor, but *you* are to provide justice.

By following these laws they were to become a *counter-cultural* presence, an *alternative* or *contrast* community. Why did God tell them not to murder or defraud each other or take each other's wives? Why did God enforce things like rest and debt cancellation? Why did God promise to personally dwell among them?

So they wouldn't look like everyone else.

And why did God want them not to look like everyone else? Because everyone else's lives were built on lies, idolatry, and injustice. Because in and through his peculiar people, God was doing something about the way Sin had maimed creation. Because God wanted the rest of the world to look at them and say, "Now *that* is how life is supposed to be lived. Their God is the real deal. How can I get some of whatever they have?"

Shortly after Steve Jobs returned to Apple in 1997, he knew they needed to refresh not only the business model and product, but also their identity. So they launched a new marketing campaign centered on the phrase "Think Different." Remember the posters featuring cultural standouts like Einstein, Gandhi, Lennon, Dylan, Picasso, and King? Remember the commercials built around the following statement?

Here's to the crazy ones. The misfits. The rebels. The troublemakers. The round pegs in the square holes. The ones who see things differently. They're not fond of rules. And they have no respect for the status quo. You can quote them, disagree with them, glorify or vilify them. About the only thing you can't do is ignore them. Because they change things. They push the human race forward. And while some may see them as the crazy ones, we see genius. Because the people who are crazy enough to think they can change the world are the ones who do.[4]

Knowing who you are is crucial, especially when you're not like everyone else. And we are called to "Live Different." We have been set apart as an alternative community for the special purpose of continuing God's mission by walking in the ways of Jesus.

Speaking of whom, Paul continues by locating his readers *in Colossae* and *in Christ*. Geographically they are *in Colossae*. This is where they live and work and sleep and drink wine and make babies. It is their home. It is their theater for mission. It is the place God wants them. But it nevertheless represents a temptation to forget that they are also and more fundamentally *in Christ*. He is where they live and work and sleep and drink wine and make babies.

You and I don't live in Colossae because Colossae is buried under centuries of compacted earth. However, you live somewhere, and that somewhere is your home. You are *in* Vegas or Valencia or Virginia Beach. This is your theater for mission. But it also represents a temptation toward spiritual amnesia. Wherever you are, never forget that you don't fully belong. Paul's greeting reminds us that wherever our somewhere happens to be, here in this place we are called to be different.

Essentially, what Paul teaches us is that in order to be faithful to Jesus, we must get used to the fact that we're going to be weird. You've got to accept that you're not going to look like everyone around you. You will define failure and success differently. How you treat your neighbors and even your enemies will come across as strange. What you do or don't do with your body will not be normal.

Growing up I was taught that although we are *in* the world we are not to be *of* it. In other words, not characterized by its habits or values. These prepositions are helpful, as are others such as *for* and *against*. We are for the

---

[4] To read more about this commercial and the transition it symbolized, see Walter Isaacson, *Steve Jobs* (New York: Simon & Schuster, 2011), 327-339.

world, but being for it sometimes requires that we come against it, for instance when exposing evils like sexual immorality, substance addiction, or political idolatry.

So we are *for* this world we are *in* by not being *of* it and at times coming *against* it. Which means following Jesus may make you feel alone, misunderstood, and different.

Here's to the holy ones.

Hope
Chapter 2 – Colossians 1.3-5a

Paul's answer to our disappointment is hope.

> *We give thanks to the God and Father of our Lord Jesus Christ in all our prayers for you, having heard of your faith in Christ Jesus and the love you have for all those set apart, a faith and love based on the hope that is safely reserved for you in heaven.*   – Colossians 1.3-5a

Faith, hope, and love quickly became the core of early Christian spirituality. In another place Paul famously draws attention to love as "the greatest" of the three (1 Corinthians 13.13). But here love gets back-paged in favor of hope. Here Paul sets hope apart as the anchor for both faith and love. Hope is fundamental. Hope is foundational. Hope is the key.

Why do you think Paul puts so much emphasis on *hope*? This is hardly the only time he talks about it. Of the 84 times we find the word hope in the New Testament, 55 come from his pen. Maybe it's because his résumé includes the following:

> I have worked much harder, been in prison more frequently, been flogged more severely, and been exposed to death again and again. Five times I received from the Jews the forty lashes minus one. Three times I was beaten with rods, once I was pelted with stones, three times I was

18

shipwrecked, I spent a night and a day in the open sea, I have been constantly on the move. I have been in danger from rivers, in danger from bandits, in danger from my fellow Jews, in danger from Gentiles; in danger in the city, in danger in the country, in danger at sea; and in danger from false believers. I have labored and toiled and have often gone without sleep; I have known hunger and thirst and have often gone without food; I have been cold and naked. Besides everything else, I face daily the pressure of my concern for all the churches. Who is weak, and I do not feel weak? Who is led into sin, and I do not inwardly burn?   – 2 Corinthians 11.23-29

Maybe Paul spotlights hope because he's writing to people who know pain. Colossians speaks to folks who aren't numb enough to ignore the fact that even with Christ, life isn't perfect. Paul addresses those who want *more.* Why do they want more? Because they ache. Because they thirst. Because they hurt. Because they're disappointed.

Hope is the language of pain, after all. Hope means frighteningly little to someone whose life is fine. Why do you think in another letter Paul emphasizes that hope does not disappoint? Because by the time you get to hope, everything else has.

Think about this question for a minute: What does hope do?

On the surface, the answer is obvious. Hope focuses us on the future – on a better tomorrow that changes our perspective today. Sometimes in the Bible hope refers to the feeling of confidently waiting for something. But here Paul isn't talking about the feeling of hope. He's talking about the content of hope. He's talking about eternal life with God. He reminds us that a day will come when God will heal all creation, when heaven will come down and God will dwell with us on a renewed earth. Paul speaks of a future day when we will be fully liberated from the painful effects of sin, Satan, and death on our bodies, souls, and communities. Hope reminds us that the story isn't over yet, that we're living out the plot rather than enjoying final resolution.

Let's dig a bit deeper though. What, by focusing us on the future, does hope *do*? How does hope impact us? What difference does it make?

To be quite honest, most of the time I find hope incredibly frustrating. Why? Because I want immediate relief.

Hope exposes my demand for immediate relief. For the healing of all my wounds and the solving of all my problems *today*. For my best life *now*. I don't want to hurt, and I don't want to see others hurt. I'd rather not accept brokenness or pain. More to the point, I'd rather not accept God's patient way of mending brokenness and overcoming pain. Sometimes I think heaven is kind of a copout. I'm a fixer and I *will* find a solution.

You and I probably aren't too different. So what do we do? Since we can't live without hope, we reinvent it. We create our own hopes. False hopes.

We invent the false secular hope of solving every problem through technology and reason. Who among us isn't preoccupied with finding quick, easy, and reasonable solutions? Practice these principles and get along great with your teenage children! Follow this technique and make millions within three years! Apply this method to guarantee a marriage filled with great conversation *and* great sex!

We invent the false spiritual hope of securing inner peace by tapping the power of now, learning to fall in love with ourselves, or unleashing the divine spark within.

We invent so many false political hopes I don't even know which one to pick on.

We invent the false pseudo-Christian hope that says if we only pray this prayer, speak in this tongue, adopt this attitude, or have a little more faith, then God will give us the Disneyland experience we want to think he's promised.

We either replace Jesus or supplement him to get what we've previously decided we deserve. Supplementing Jesus with the right formula typically reveals a failure to come to terms with the fundamental reality that our pain won't completely disappear this side of eternity.

The Colossian Christians started strong with Jesus, pledging their lives to his kingdom and coming to experience previously unknown joys like forgiveness and freedom in him. But as time wore on and disappointment set in, they wondered. We're good with Jesus, but maybe there's room for more? Jesus has helped our pursuit of the good life, but maybe "everything we need" is a bit too much to ask?

Surely you've asked yourself the same questions. Surely you've considered that somewhere out there you might find something better or deeper or more.

They were glancing elsewhere, and we only look elsewhere when staying *here* feels like missing out. Now as then, we don't have to look far for people claiming a new brand of spirituality – a new brand of hope – that marginalizes Jesus. They may not reject Jesus completely. More likely they add to him. Maybe they even consider themselves Jesus-followers, but they mix their faith in Christ with competing trusts and allegiances.

We're talking about a Jesus-plus or a Jesus-and kind of hope. Sure, you can have your Jesus, but how about a little astrology too? Jesus is great for Sundays and the kids, but on Monday business reopens and it's time to follow the real experts. Jesus can have "religion," but leave society to those who get paid to run the world.

Paul gently warns us that Jesus-plus is a broken hope. Jesus-and is just another demand for the immediate relief God simply hasn't promised us this side of eternity. Jesus-and only puts more time between you and the realization that (a) only God can repair what's gone wrong with the world and (b) his rescue operation will take longer than we'd prefer.

Hope exposes our demand for immediate relief.

But our demand isn't only rooted in rebellion. It's rooted in pain. Mature people who know God will see the world for what it is – a breathtaking, glorious, horrifying place. And not just breathtaking, glorious, and horrifying, but also incomplete. Behind our demand for satisfaction is a cry for God to fix us. We are not okay and we know it.

Hope reminds us that for right now pain is normal. Hope gives us permission to hurt. If we weren't disappointed now, then nothing better would be on the way. Hope frees us to admit that as much as we have to be thankful for, sometimes the world still fails. If the world didn't hurt, we wouldn't need hope. But it does. And we do. Maybe a prerequisite for knowing the power of hope is acknowledging the depth of our pain.

What does hope do? Hope exposes our demandingness. Hope permits our disappointment. But most importantly, we must never forget, hope assures us that our pain won't last forever. The happy ending of our story is as certain as God himself. Paul underscores the security of hope, which is not slippery or vulnerable to attack. On the contrary, it is *safely reserved for us in heaven* – the place that houses all the stuff no one can mess with.

Hope reminds us that God *has* promised complete healing, total transformation, and full relief. Just not yet.

Gospel
Chapter 3 – Colossians 1.3-5a

Why should you care about the gospel?

You already care about so much: your husband's job, your wife's health, your children's activities and future, your education, your portfolio, your golf game, your holiday boutique, your parents, your calorie intake, your computer, your dog. Caring takes time. Caring takes energy. Caring is hard. So why make room to care about the gospel?

Do you ever notice how seriously the Bible's authors take what they're talking about? I think about this with all of Paul's letters, but especially Galatians. I know we're studying Colossians, but bear with me for a minute. In both cases some person or group of people were trying to supplement Jesus. They were adding-on to the gospel, and by adding to it they were changing it. And changing the gospel was the surest way to get a rise out of Paul.

I don't know if you know this, but Paul was short and probably bald. So when you read this quote from Galatians 1.6-10, picture a short, bald, exasperated Jewish guy whose forehead is redder than Rudolph's nose and who talks so intensely he keeps spitting on the folks up front:

I am astonished that you are so quickly deserting the one who called you to live in the grace of Christ and are turning to a different gospel — which is really no gospel at all. Evidently some people are throwing you into confusion and are trying to pervert the gospel of Christ. But even if we or an angel from heaven should preach a gospel other than the one we preached to you, let them be under God's curse! As we have already said, so now I say again: If anybody is preaching to you a gospel other than what you accepted, let them be under God's curse!

The troublemakers in Galatia were telling Jesus-followers that they needed to obey Jesus *plus* the Law of Moses, and to be circumcised as a way of accepting this task. Later in the letter Paul mockingly suggests that they "go the whole way and emasculate themselves!" (Gal 6.12). Intense, right?! I told you this stuff matters to him. But this just brings us back to the question of why. Why does Paul care so much about the gospel? Why should the Colossians? Why should we?

Very quickly in Colossians Paul roots his hearers squarely in the gospel.

*We give thanks . . . having heard of your faith in Christ Jesus and the love you have for all those set apart, a faith and love based on the hope that is safely reserved for you in heaven. This you previously heard about in the true message of the **gospel**.* — Colossians 1.3-4

Blink and you'll miss it, but don't let the lack of fanfare fool you. Paul mentions the gospel here and in 1.23, forming what's called an *inclusio*. By bracketing the opening section of his letter in this way, Paul drops a hint that everything in between unwraps what the gospel is all about.

So tell me: When you hear the word "gospel," what comes to mind?

Maybe you think about street preachers; a certain style of music; Matthew, Mark, Luke, and John; or Jesus dying for your sins. Play the same game in Paul's world and most folks would say "Rome" or "Caesar" or "*Pax Romana.*" *Pax Romana* was a popular saying in Paul's day that claimed the gods had called the Romans to spread peace and justice all over the world. This belief gained ground with the reforms of Rome's first emperor, Caesar Augustus. He governed the Roman Empire for most of Jesus' life and his legacy became intimately associated with the idea of "gospel."[5]

---

[5] See Neil Elliott and Mark Reasoner, *Documents and Images for the Study of Paul* (Downers Grove: IVP, 2011), 119-174.

23

Gospel is a mostly a religious term today, but back then it stemmed just as much from the political realm. Gospel basically meant "good news" and involved announcing a victory or the birth of someone destined to reign. Think "Extra, extra, read all about it!" combined with "Four score and seven years ago."

With these things in mind, check out this inscription from 9 BC.

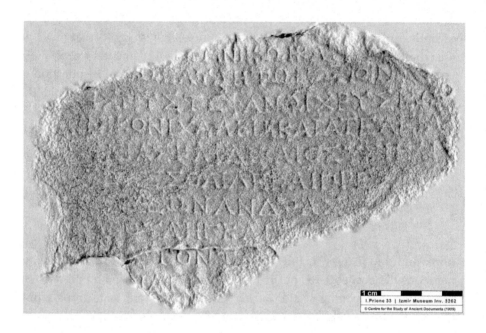

You're looking at Greek letters imprinted onto a piece of stone. Here's what it says in English:

> Since Providence, which has ordered all things and is deeply interested in our life, has set things in most perfect order by giving us Augustus, whom she filled with virtue that he might benefit humankind, sending him as a Savior, both for us and for our descendants, that he might end war and arrange all things. And since he, Caesar, by his appearance excelled even our anticipations, surpassing all previous benefactors, and not even leaving to posterity any hope of surpassing what he has done, and *since the birthday of the god Augustus was the beginning of the good news for the world* that came by reason of him.

A little wordy, I know. But did you notice the connection between "gospel" (here translated *good news*) and Caesar Augustus? Earlier in the same document, the author suggested resetting the calendar so that Year One corresponds to Augustus' birth, "so one may rightly take this day as the time when the beginning of existence and life has come to be, which is the limit and end for any regret that one has been born." Did you catch that? Through Augustus a new age has dawned. Only after his arrival was being born reason for cheers rather than tears!

Why in the world would someone say these things? This wasn't just an isolated incident, either. An entire faith flourished around devotion to the Roman emperors. We've all seen folks scream in delight or weep with joy when their preferred candidate wins the Presidential election, but even we don't get this excited.

But Augustus was special. He overcame every obstacle and enemy that stood between most Romans and the good life they desired for themselves and their children. He brought peace to a land ravaged by decades of civil war. He cleansed the sea of pirates, defeated border-threatening barbarians, and returned runaway slaves to their masters. He offered grace to conquered foes, streamlined the government, and enlarged the boundaries of the empire. He even renewed patriotic fervor by restoring traditional Roman morality as a way of regaining favor from the gods. (He didn't exactly follow his own moral guidelines, but that's another story!) And after securing empire-wide stability, he humbly handed power back to the Roman people.

This would be like our next President cutting unemployment in half, solving the energy crisis, presenting a workable health care solution supported by both parties, establishing incorruptible governments in Uganda and the Sudan, and finally bringing peace in places like Pakistan and North Korea – all while eliminating our national debt *and* lowering taxes across the board. Who wouldn't love an overcomer like that?!

It's no wonder Romans praised Augustus and his descendants with the title *Divi Filius* or "son of a god." How else could you explain such a dream come true?

And therein lies the core of what gospel is all about. Who has turned dream into reality? Who has overcome? Who has won the victories necessary to sustain our well-being? Who has defeated our enemies and liberated us from the prison that life so often becomes? Who has acted on behalf of God (or the gods) to bring peace and justice for all?

Paul disagreed with the standard Roman answer. He took issue with the gospel of Rome in part because he saw the truth that *Pax Romana* meant peace and justice only for those at the top. But mostly Paul rejected such propaganda because he knew the God in whose presence even powerful nations are like drops of water in a bucket or dust so weightless no scale would recognize its presence (see Isaiah 40.15-17).

Paul believed in and preached an alternative gospel that declared the surprising victory of an altogether different Savior and Lord.

Why? When he was facing such incomprehensible odds, what so possessed Paul that he believed in, preached, taught, fought for, and eventually lost his head because of this gospel?

I'll tell you why. Because Paul's gospel fulfilled God's promises to win God's victory and establish God's kingdom. Because this gospel centers on something, or rather *someone*, found nowhere else. You can probably guess what possessed this insufferable little mountain of balding bearded man: Jesus.

Paul will spend this entire letter reminding us what we so often forget. What Jesus has accomplished makes Augustus' achievements look silly. And you can replace "Augustus" with whomever or whatever you think makes the world go round. Only Jesus has overcome everything that stands between us and the life for which we so desperately dream. Only Jesus lived a spotless life and offered himself as a sacrifice for our sins. Only Jesus absorbed evil's heaviest blow and nevertheless emerged victorious. Only Jesus reversed Adam's curse. Only Jesus defeated death. Only Jesus modeled true life. Only Jesus ushered in the kingdom of God. Here at the beginning, Paul sort of teases us by mentioning the gospel without unpacking it. I don't want to spoil the fun either, so at this point I won't say much more than him.

Why should we care about the gospel of Jesus?

I think by the end you'll be asking a different question: Why not?

Truth
Chapter 4 – Colossians 1.5-8

Do you know any "big fish" storytellers? You know, the kind of people who can observe a robin making a nest, see in their mind a hawk writing poetry, and relay the tale as a giant eagle saving the world from nuclear disaster?

I get that feeling when I read Paul's letters. He talks so . . . big. One people called out from among the rest to redeem creation. Hope powerful enough to sustain faith and love even in a world of racism and slavery. The gospel of God saving us all through a virgin-born Jewish carpenter from Nazareth. How absurd? How scandalous? How strange can you get?

Paul's letter arrived in Colossae under the arm of his letter-carrying assistant Tychicus, and as soon as Tychicus showed up, the churches gathered to hear him read and explain it. He's just getting started, but can't you already hear the murmurs? Can't you imagine the more critical hearers mumbling questions and objections to Paul's claims?

The *gospel* of *Jesus*? Really, Paul? I mean, we too once believed that Jesus was more powerful, more life-giving, and more legit than everything else on offer – including Rome herself. We too once fell into what now looks like a trap – the trap of thinking Jesus marked the end of our search for fulfillment, for guidance, for the Divine. But haven't we grown beyond all this? Isn't it obvious that Jesus is at best one player in the game? Have you not yet come to terms with the hard reality that hope is an illusion, that your gospel has run aground, that Jesus isn't everything you think he is?

Two thousand years have only added to the volume and intensity of our criticisms. We don't mind having Jesus around, but relax with the "he is everything we need" stuff. Certainly time has demonstrated the inability of Jesus to make a unique and lasting difference in the world. And surely we've evolved beyond the wishful thinking of *hope*. Do we not now see "hope" for what it is – nothing more than our projection onto a dreamy future what we've accepted we can't have here and now? Stop denying reality. Life in this world is hard and filled with pain. End of story. Deal with it. The "gospel" of Jesus proved to be nothing but one more failed attempt by horses and men to put humpty-dumpty together again. Get over it. Move on.

Or so we sometimes think.

It's not that we've turned our backs on faith. Hardly! Most of us admit that regardless of its actual basis, faith is pretty useful in the 21st century. God tempers the ambitions of those hungry for power. Faith gives poor people something to believe in. Religion keeps the kids in line.

If you've never seen a witty British comedian travel all fifty states in search of what makes America so American, you should watch *Stephen Fry in America*. Among the many places he visited – including ex- atomic bomb shelters and a voodoo party – the most revealing conversation about faith came at the notorious Angola State Penitentiary in rural Louisiana.

Proud of reforming a 5000-inmate, 18,000-acre, violence-ridden, drug-infested, gang-driven wasteland into a place of relative peace and restoration, prison warden Burl Caine explained the role of faith in keeping prisoners in line: "We don't care what religion. We just look for morality. It's real simple in life: moral people aren't criminals. They don't rape, pillage, and steal. So if we can change inmates to be moral people, we've really rehabilitated them."

Notice how "religion" isn't valued for its own sake or because it's true, but because it *works*, because it serves some greater purpose. Generally speaking, that's how our culture views faith. Figure out what we need to do – stabilize society, grow our churches, fix our families – and find a brand of religion that helps. Doesn't matter which faith, so long as it serves us well.

This way of thinking is a legitimate temptation for many of us. Why? Because we want to make a difference. And because we don't *want* to be exclusive; we don't *want* to tell other people we think they're wrong. But Paul doesn't let us off the hook so easily. It's not that he wants us to be spiteful or arrogant, or that he thinks God doesn't care about society or family, but neither does he willingly surrender the question of *truth*.

Twice in Colossians 1.5-8 Paul draws attention to the *truth* of what we believe.

*This you previously heard about in the **true** message of the gospel, which has come to you just as in all the world it is bearing fruit and growing. It has done the same thing in you from the first day you heard about and came to know the **truth** of God's grace, as you learned it from Epaphras our beloved fellow bondslave.*

The increasingly popular "True for you but not for me" won't work in this case. Most brands of faith in the first century Roman Empire had no problem making room for one another. In their quest for bountiful crops or transcendent experiences, why not enlist the assistance of as many deities as you can find (or invent)? The more the merrier, so long as you don't threaten the glory of Rome. In this world both Judaism and Christianity were labeled "atheists" for refusing to believe in multiple gods.

Talking about "truth" in matters of faith won't win many friends in our world, either. Yet here we have Paul – here we have our Bibles – doing just that. To call the gospel "truth" is to say that it's genuine, trustworthy, reliable. A true message lines up with reality and communicates the way things really are – not just how we'd like them to be, or how we say they are in order to serve some parental or political purpose.

This is also the only place Paul talks about "conversion" as *learning* the gospel. Usually he speaks of folks trusting in or hearing or obeying the gospel, but not learning. He also specifically describes this message as something they *came to know* or *understood*. They thought hard, weighed all the possibilities, and perceived the truthfulness of what they were hearing.

Do you notice what Paul is doing? He's reminding them that they didn't cry their way into the faith or jump on board for material benefits. Most of them suffered rejection from family and business associates when they acknowledged Jesus as Lord. Yet when Epaphras systematically laid out the claims of Jesus and the gospel of the apostles, they responded. Paul does not say, "Remember when you were moved by the Spirit and accepted Jesus into your heart?" He says, "Remember when Epaphras presented you with a clear explanation of the faith, and you said, 'Yes!' You believed this was more than just wonderful. You believed this was true."

Paul isn't trying to *convince* the Colossians of anything. He's merely *reminding* them of what they already know, or at least what they previously came to believe. Paul refused to believe in multiple gods and their various gospels, and so had his friends in Colossae. Paul believed he had found the truth, or rather that the Truth had found him. So did they. So have we.

What if what Paul says is true actually is? Don't forget what he's talking about: the gospel, hope, grace. Imagine he's right. Imagine Jesus really died and God really raised him from the dead. What if through him God really has dealt with our sins, defeated death, and set us on a path toward real life starting today and stretching into eternity? What if hope is rooted not in fantasy but in the fulfillment of all God's promises? What if God is reliable? What if God's anger has given way to mercy? What if God looks at you not with fury or irritation but with grace? What if he sees you and smiles?

The question is not whether you live with answers to these questions. The question is whether your answers can be trusted. The question is not whether you believe a version of the Truth. The question is whether your version of Truth is true.

Paul isn't demanding that we agree with him. He's asking us to let him remind us why we once did. I'm not asking you to tattoo TRUTH on your forearm and shove the gospel down the throat of everyone you meet. I'm asking you to remember *that* you believe, and keep reading so we can remind you *what* you believe.

I think you'll find once again that it is more than just wonderful.

Movement
Chapter 5 – Colossians 1.5-8

Does being a "Christian" ever feel small to you? Or random? Or weak?

Paul always believed in a big God. Yet the Colossians were tiny and they knew it. Of all the cities Paul worked with, Colossae was by far the least significant.

Paul also believed in a purposeful God. Yet the Colossians could look around and wonder at what seemed like the randomness of it all: "My neighbor Nicanor worships at the feet of Zeus, my cousin Julius at the temple of Apollo, my parents dabble in magic and astrology, and all of them burn incense to the emperor. What makes Jesus so special?"

While Paul's God didn't always make sense to finite human minds, neither was this God emotionally manipulative. But maybe the Colossians, like so many others since, looked back on their "conversion" and saw nothing more than an irrational decision prompted more by momentary emotions than mature evaluation.

Do you ever think these things? Do you ever wonder if you love God simply because your parents did and you're falling in line, or simply because they didn't and you're running the opposite direction? Are you haunted by the prospect that faith is nothing more than psychological wish-fulfillment or political propaganda invented to keep people under control? Do you fear that you follow Jesus because it just so happened that you grew up in America or Uganda or Brazil?

No one can deny that since the first century, Christianity has been on the move. But movements come and go. What about this one deserves your enduring allegiance?

In Colossians 1.5-8, Paul calls our attention to the fact that we're part of a movement.

This you previously heard about in the true message of the gospel, which has come to you just as in all the world it is bearing fruit and growing. It has done the same thing in you from the first day you heard about and came to know the truth of God's grace, as you learned it from Epaphras our beloved fellow bondslave. He is faithful on our behalf as a servant of Christ; he also made clear to us your love in the Spirit.

Let's break what he says down into three facts we too easily forget.

(1) The movement you've joined is not random. We sometimes struggle to see what makes faith different from other preference decisions we make every day. No one cares if you choose Speed Stick over Axe or Old Spice. One man's scent is another man's stink, depending on whose nose you're trying to impress. Today's religious menu easily rivals the deodorant aisle for sheer variety of options. Is anything more at stake? Could you just as sensibly become an atheist or a Buddhist as remain a Christian?

Paul's world provided every bit as many paths, yet he proudly assures us that in Christ we've found something special – and not just special, but purposeful. Here, he says, we see the realizing of God's dream for creation.

Most of us probably missed this, so let's take another look. Paul says the gospel message had reached Colossae *just as in all the world it is bearing fruit and growing.* Remind you of anything?

God's first command to Adam and Eve was simple: "*Be fruitful and increase* in number. Fill the earth and subdue it" (Genesis 1.28). Apparently God didn't have to tell them twice, because they started making babies right away. But not until after they maimed God's creation project by rejecting God and going their own way. Naturally things went from bad to unbearable, so God decided to scrap it all and start over with Noah and his family. They received a similar command: "Be fruitful and increase in number; multiply on the earth and increase upon it" (Gen 9.7). You may have heard that Noah didn't fare much better than Adam, but God refused to quit. Determined to fix what humanity shattered, God promised

Abraham a family who would become God's way of saving the world. Problem was, Abraham had no kids. After a few false starts, God told Abraham, "I will make you very fruitful; I will make nations of you, and kings will come from you" (Genesis 17.6).

Be fruitful. Increase. Grow. Multiply. With this in mind, remember what Paul told the Colossians. The true gospel has reached you *just as in all the world it is bearing fruit and growing.*

Now does this remind you of anything? God told Adam, Abraham, and Noah to be *fruitful*, to *grow* and *increase* to *fill the earth*. And the gospel of Jesus was doing just that! I know Paul talks funny, so let me restate his point: The entire story of God peaks in Jesus. The gospel of Jesus fulfills what God has been doing since the beginning.

When you decided to walk in the ways of Jesus, you didn't randomly choose one option among an aisle of equals. You stepped back into the story you were created to live. You may have thought that you were making God part of your story. No offense, but you were wrong. When you said yes to Jesus, God edited back into his story the role you were literally born to play.

Paul's claim is heavy, to say the least! But simply saying you're something special hardly means you've lived up to the billing. I can *say* that the gospel of Jesus fulfills God's purposes for creation, but why should you agree?

(2) The movement you've joined is not small. Colossae was small, and the church in Colossae was smaller. We're talking about maybe two or three house churches of no more than thirty-five to fifty people each. At best that totals 150 people from among the 100,000-150,000 Colossians in mid-first century AD. Like I said, small. While the Colossians may have felt that a good look around exposed proud claims about Jesus as silly, Paul reminded them that they were part of something bigger than what they could see.

Here and again in Colossians 1.23, Paul lets them in on a little secret: the gospel is everywhere. Paul wrote this letter while under house arrest in Rome, which just so happened to be the center of the known world. All roads led not only *to* Rome, but also *from* Rome back to homes all across the land. The gospel had reached the known world's epicenter, and it was only getting started. Paul may not have known at the time just how much ground the gospel still had to cover, but what for him was rhetorical hyperbole is for us nearly established fact.

The gospel is everywhere.

You do realize, don't you, that Christianity is hardly an American phenomenon. Matter of fact, right now you'd have a better chance of believing in Jesus if you lived in many parts of Asia, Africa, or South America. As growth has slowed here in the Land of the Free (and certainly among our European ancestors), Christianity is exploding in the South and East. Here's what you need to remember: All kinds of people put their faith in Jesus every day. Rich people. Poor people. Tall people. Short people. Needy people. Healthy people. Bad people. Good people. Estimates suggest that over 80,000 people will become Jesus-followers today, and most of them don't look anything like you.[6] The gospel is as global as it gets.

(3) The movement you've joined is not impotent. Christianity was global before global was cool. But living in the Internet Age, we're hardly unique in this sense. Coca-Cola is just as difficult to outrun as Jesus, but who cares? Sure it increases our global sugar intake and makes someone somewhere a lot of money, but in spite of advertising attempts to convince us otherwise, Coke doesn't actually transform people for the better.

Conversely, the authentic gospel changes lives everywhere it goes.

If you read the introduction, you know Epaphras as Paul's co-worker who first brought the news about Jesus to Colossae. He was a church-planter, a pioneer, and a teacher. But for many Colossians, this only told the second half of his story. They knew him as a boy. They knew his ex-girlfriends and his old drinking buddies. They remembered how he left Colossae a devout worshiper of Roman gods and goddesses, yet returned as a worshiper of a convicted backwoods Galilean named Jesus. Of course I'm speculating a bit, but not much. His name was short for "Epaphroditus," which means he was named for Aphrodite, the famous pagan goddess of love. He wasn't exactly raised to love Jesus.

The Colossians knew Epaphras as a changed man, and for that matter they knew the same of themselves. They couldn't deny that God's Spirit had worked in them a love for one another and for other Jesus-followers such as Paul, whom they had never even met.

This movement you've joined bears a surprising purpose, scope, and power. What the gospel is doing in you, the gospel is doing all over the world. What the gospel is doing all over the world, the gospel is doing

---

[6] Kimberly Gray, "Around the World There are More Christians," *Abilene Reporter-News* http://www.reporternews.com/news/2010/jul/22/around-world-more-christians. Accessed 4/20/12.

wherever you are. And what the gospel is doing here, there, and everywhere, is *growing* in numbers and *bearing the fruit* of transformed lives built on faith, anchored by hope, and demonstrated in love.

Future
Chapter 6 – Colossians 1.9-12a

Picture yourself as the parent of a 22-year old soon-to-be college graduate. Imagine you've raised a good kid – intelligent, hardworking, socially engaged, kind. Three-and-a-half years ago he enrolled in the local university in pursuit of a degree. But today that same child stands in the middle of your kitchen informing you that he's done with school and plans to walk away with only one semester left.

What do you do? You probably give him the "Here is where you are headed if you stay the course" speech. You remind him that he's never been a quitter. You clarify that while college degrees don't include guarantees, young applicants with the right wall decorations still make 25-40% more on that fact alone. You suggest that in twenty years he won't want to explain to colleagues how he *almost* finished college. You mention that a full-time job and a family will make it harder to go back, if indeed he decides to finish.

You're not reprimanding and you're not simply reproducing a list of pros and cons. You are painting a picture of what his life could become if he stays.

In today's text, Paul tries to persuade the Colossians not to move on from Jesus. Someone has suggested that while Jesus fulfills some of their needs and answers some of their questions, Christ alone isn't enough. There's no need to write him out of their past, but the future demands something more.

Paul wants *more* for them too, not less. But it is more rooted in what they already have. It is more progress along the same road, not more in the sense of a different path or even a detour from this one. It's great to want more. It just needs to be the right kind of more. The wrong kind of more may feel like more for a minute, but in the end it always turns out to be less.

To move on from Jesus is to move away from Jesus, and to move away from Jesus is to miss out on the future God has planned for you. Paul portrays this future in Colossians 1.9-14:

> *Because of this, from the first day we heard about you we have not stopped praying for you and asking that you be filled with the knowledge of God's will in all Spiritual wisdom and understanding, so that you may walk in a manner worthy of the Lord that pleases him in every way: bearing fruit in every kind of good work and growing in the knowledge of God, being strengthened with all power according to the might of his glory so you always have endurance and patience, joyfully giving thanks to the Father.*

God once promised his people he had good plans for them – a hope and a future – so long as they kept the faith (Jeremiah 29.11). Paul issues a similar promise. You can become this kind of person if you don't dilute your loyalty to Jesus.

Notice the talk of *fulfillment*, as well as the emphasis on *every, always,* and *all*. Why look elsewhere when everything you need can be found right here? That's what Paul thinks, but do you agree?

One time I was driving to a wedding in the middle of nowhere. They told me to turn right at the stoplight and keep going until I saw balloons about 200 feet off the road. But it was getting dark, and balloons never stand out as much as people think. Did I make a wrong turn somewhere? Maybe I should turn around and go back the way I came. Was I on the right road but had already passed the balloons? Maybe I should just go home. (Oh wait, I'm officiating the wedding.)

Turns out the balloons were farther than I imagined and I just needed to keep moving forward. (Gotta love those awkwardly-and-yet-surprisingly-helpfully-placed gas stations.) Thankfully I arrived on time, though not exactly in a festive mood. Being lost is even more frustrating when you know you're close.

Here we see Paul as a convenience store clerk saying, "Everything is all right, just drive a bit further down the road. Keep on going the same direction and you'll get there, I promise." Or to continue with our original metaphor, today's text is Paul's "This is where you are headed if you stay the course" speech. This is what's in store for us if we stare straight ahead and keep moving forward.

Before we go any further, notice that Paul envisions our promised future while *praying*. By painting through prayer Paul reminds us that (a) what he prays will come to pass as surely as God is faithful, and (b) what comes to pass will not be our own doing but the work of God's Spirit in us. Here is what God will do, Paul says, if you stop getting in his way. I'm not sure this is what the Queen had in mind when she told Alice, "It's a poor sort of memory that only works backwards," but it definitely fits. Paul reminds us of our future to provide encouragement in the present.

Let's flesh out Paul's prayer one bit at a time. First, he prays that his readers *be filled with the knowledge of God's will in all Spiritual wisdom and understanding.* Knowledge, wisdom, and understanding are synonyms that could also be translated insight, discernment, or comprehension. The surface meaning is clear: God's Spirit will teach us how to live. We will learn to discern what God wants and to put that knowledge into practice.

Knowledge, wisdom, and understanding represented the highest moral ideals of philosophers in Paul's day (who followed the teachings of famous thinkers like Socrates, Plato, and Aristotle). Perhaps more importantly for Paul, they also recall Old Testament descriptions of the good life God desired for his chosen ones. "For the LORD gives wisdom; from his mouth come knowledge and understanding. He holds success in store for the upright, he is a shield to those whose walk is blameless" (Proverbs 2.6-7; also check out Exodus 31.1-4 and Isaiah 11.2).

In other words, the best anyone in your world hopes for will be yours. You will know all you need and be all you can be, always to the end *that you may walk in a manner worthy of the Lord that pleases him in every way.*

What does it mean to walk in a manner worthy of the Lord and please him in every way? Thankfully, Paul brushes four more strokes:

Bearing fruit in every kind of good work. If you stay the course, the gospel will do in you what it is doing all over the world. Your life will become one story after another of doing good and making a difference in the lives of people around you.

Growing in the knowledge of God. If you keep walking the same direction, you won't just know God's *will* better. You'll actually know God himself better. You and God will develop an ever-increasing friendship.

Being strengthened with all power according to the might of his glory so you always have endurance and patience. If you drive just a bit further, you'll become the kind of person who can't be thrown off course. Paul seems to pile up the terms here: strength, power, might, glory. The net effect is that you'll be unshakeable. Overwhelming situations? You'll enjoy endurance in abundance. Difficult people? You'll have patience to spare.

Joyfully giving thanks to the Father. If you don't stop now, want to know what's coming your way? Joy. The kind of joy that flows naturally from an actively grateful awareness of all that you have and all that you are. In other words, you won't just not be sorry. You'll be so glad you stuck with Jesus that your mouth will virtually open itself and constantly remind the rest of you how much you have to be thankful for.

Do you want to belong to a community known for doing all kinds of good? Do you want to be a person who interacts with God personally and intelligently? Are you interested in being stable enough that nothing and no one can shake you? Do you desire a life so full that gratitude flows freely from within? If you've answered yes to any or all of these questions, then do not turn to the right or left because you are already headed in the right direction.

Redemption
Chapter 7 – Colossians 1.12-14

Do you ever feel stuck in your own story?

People visit my office every week with no idea what to make of the mess they've made with the one life they've been given. So I ask to hear their story. Wayward children. Overbearing parents. Broken promises. Icy marriages. Floundering careers. Hidden addictions. Shattered dreams. All clichés, to be sure. But clichés hurt quite a bit when you're living them.

When our stories regress into the realm of painful cliché, we forget. "I wish we could just go back to the way it used to be." Really? If the way it used to be was so wonderful and healthy, you wouldn't be where you are now. And you probably weren't complaining any less back then.

When today becomes unbearable or boring, we misremember. "Looking back I think I never really loved her." Seriously? No offense, but that's dumb. Of course you loved her. You just can't remember what it felt like so you're rewriting history to match how you feel right now.

So we've spent the past week exercising our memory muscle. We've let Paul guide us back to the beginning, to the foundation, to the history of how and why we came to consider ourselves people who believe in and belong to Jesus.

As he rounds out this section and prepares for what comes next, he closes his penultimate paragraph on a high note: thanksgiving. Paul actually encourages thankfulness more in Colossians than any of his other letters.

Why? Because when we're tempted to move on from Jesus, or to supplement him with a pinch of this and a dash of that, we need to remember what God has done for us and say thanks.

When is the last time you stopped and thought about what God has done for you?

We spend most of our time thinking about what we have to do. Task lists and errands and such. If we do think about God, we generally think about what we want or need from him as we go about this business. If we do reflect on what God has given us, we typically thank him for earthly blessings we now enjoy. All this is normal and good. Obviously we've got things we must do. Clearly God has invited us to bring all our requests before him. Certainly God wants us to acknowledge that all good things come from him.

But there's more. So much more.

Let's rephrase the question: When is the last time you pushed pause and pondered the fact that God has *saved* you? When in the past year have you specifically set aside time to understand and enjoy salvation?

You're about to get a new answer to that question.

Give thanks to the Father, who has qualified us to receive a share in the inheritance of those set apart in the light, who delivered us out of the dominion of darkness and transferred us into the kingdom of his beloved Son, in whom we have redemption, the forgiveness of sins.

– Colossians 1.12-14

Before we dive into Paul's words, we need to note what lies behind what he says. Paul is rehearsing the story of God saving us from darkness, but he does so in ways that echo the story of God saving Israel from Egypt.

For 400 years God's people suffered through slavery in Egypt, exploited and abused by the arrogance of empire. They cried out to God. God heard them. "I have indeed seen your misery, heard your cry, and am concerned about your suffering," God said, "so I am coming down to rescue you and bring you out from that oppressive place to a land flowing with milk and honey" (Exodus 6.7-10). To make a long story very short, that's exactly what God did.

For ancient Jews like Jesus and Paul, the exodus story was more than just past. It was promise. For centuries, prophets had spoken of a new exodus, a day when God would again liberate his people – this time for good – from all that bound them in chains.

We believe this day has come.

Paul depicts salvation in precisely these terms. First he ensures us that we need no one else's final approval, because God himself has qualified us to receive our portion of his promised future. The language comes from the common practice of children inheriting gifts from their parents. More specifically, *share* and *inheritance* referred in the Old Testament to the land allotted to liberated Israelites (Deuteronomy 10.9; 32.9; Joshua 19.9). The underlying theme there and here is adoption. God has claimed us as his own children with all the benefits this new home brings. Orphans we were. Sons and daughters we have become. No longer hiding under the porch listening to the neighbors talking over family dinners and wondering if we'll ever belong. We will. We do.

Belonging, however, is just the beginning. Whether we knew it or not, we were living under the imperial authority of Darkness. But Darkness's license to rule has been revoked, for it is rendered powerless by the presence of Light. No longer are we unable to view things as they are. Now we see who God is, who we are, and where God is leading us. We have been rescued, and this rescue has taken the form of relocation. We have left behind our lands of oppression and been granted new citizenship in a country with no equal – the kingdom of God's own Son. Not only have we been delivered *out of* oppression, we have been transplanted *into* this land flowing with love and life and illumination.

For good measure, Paul includes two more elements of life under the reign of God's beloved Son. Redemption and forgiveness. Redemption means buying someone out of bondage and setting them on a new path toward freedom. Forgiveness involves being released from some burden so that its obligations or consequences are no longer present. The word was used in ancient Israel for release of a person from debt (as in the Jubilee laws of Leviticus 25) and in the Greek world for release from having to pay back taxes. In this case it means that the dark parts of your past don't have to ruin the rest of your story.

So as we bring this first week to a close, remember that your story is adoptable, rescuable, forgivable. No matter what. Better yet, remember that your story has already been redeemed.

Remember that though you were once orphaned and alone, now you have been grafted into a family and granted access to an inheritance that no one can take away from you. Remember that though you were once held captive by deep darkness, now you have been liberated from bondage to blindness and relocated into a kingdom of light and power and love. Remember that though you were once guilty and destined for judgment, now you have been released from the deepest consequences of your sins. Remember that though you were once abandoned into slavery, now you have been purchased by God and set free to become who you were always intended to be.

And while you're at it, remember that becoming this proverbial person-you-were-made-to-be is not just a wish or dream but a future as reliable as God is strong. Remember that your transformation – slow and tedious as it feels – plays one small part in the universal spread of the gospel throughout space and time. Remember this true and trustworthy gospel that brings hope to an arthritic world cringing under the burden of disappointment and pain. Remember who you are and how you've been designated for a higher purpose than power or pleasure or shopping or success.

And remember that all this has taken place, here, in Jesus. Who, by the way, with memory intact, we are ready to see.

MEMORY

moreJESUS part 2 – VISION

Have you ever spotted danger from the passenger seat that your driver didn't see? Or watched a foul ball sail toward someone who wasn't paying attention?

What did you do?

Unless you enjoy being in car accidents (unlikely) or watching other people get beaned (hopefully not), you probably yelled, screamed, and maybe drum-tapped the dashboard or flailed your hands for added emphasis. When we need people to notice dangers they can't currently see, we increase the volume and intensity of whatever words happen to come out of our mouths. (And there's no predicting what might come out. Is there any worse advice than "heads up" when a baseball is flying at someone's face?)

The Colossians were headed for trouble but they didn't see it. Paul saw it. They felt a pull to move on from Jesus. Paul knew that moving on from Jesus meant moving away from Jesus, and that moving away from Jesus was like texting while driving or sitting backwards at a baseball game.

But Paul was stuck under house arrest in Rome, and Colossae was 1200 miles away. All he could send was a letter, and you can't raise your voice in a letter. How do you grab someone's attention when all you have are words on a page? Since Paul apparently hadn't yet heard of emoticons, he wrote a poem. Here it is:

He is the image of the invisible God,
> *firstborn over all creation,*
>> *for in him all things were created –*
>>> *in the heavens and on earth,*
>>> *things visible and invisible,*
>>> *whether thrones or lordships or rulers or authorities.*
>> *All things have been created through him and to him,*

> *and he is before all things*
> *and in him all things hold together;*
> *and he is the head of the body, the church.*

He is the founder,
  firstborn from among the dead,
    so that in everything he might enjoy supremacy,
    for in him all the Fullness was pleased to permanently dwell,
    and through him to reconcile all things to him –
      making peace through the blood of his cross –
      whether things on earth or things in the heavens.
                                        – Colossians 1.15-20

The first thing I want you to notice about this poem is that it is a poem.[7] You write like this only if you want your readers to stop, think, scratch their heads, take a nap, wake up, pour a glass of water, and think some more. Not logic thinking. Imagination thinking. Poetry exercises our imaginations, and imagination is the muscle that enables us to see.

I might be the worst poet in the history of the world. Anytime I try to write my wife a poem, it always starts with "Roses are red, violets are purple," and then dies. But I love poetry (the really simple stuff I can understand) because I like being able to see. Poetry is about sight. Poetry has everything to do with vision. We write poetry to break open stale old perspectives and unearth fresh new ones. Much of the Bible was originally written as poetry, because the Bible is designed to help us notice what we otherwise might not see. Paul writes this poem so that we'll stop, open our eyes, and re-perceive what we might be missing.

The second thing I want you to notice about this poem is that every word is about Jesus.

This week we're going to examine Jesus through the lens provided by these verses. You know the whole forest-and-trees analogy? Think of this poem like a massive breathtaking forest. For the next six chapters we'll be hiking on ground level and examining some of the individual trees. Then on the seventh we'll step back and view everything together as a whole.

---

[7] Actually, he wrote (or quoted) what most scholars consider a hymn. But since hymns are basically poetry put to music, I'm calling it a poem. Truthfully, we can't be 100% sure if it is a poem/hymn or merely poetic/hymnic prose. What is 100% certain is that Paul never heard of emoticons. According to Wikipedia's "Emoticon" entry, the first recorded emoticon is found in the transcript of an 1862 speech by none other than Abraham Lincoln. One more reason why I love Abraham Lincoln. And Wikipedia.

I've mentioned a few times that the Colossians were being drawn away from the true gospel by a new brand of faith that promised more. Scholars can't agree about what precisely this teaching looked like, mainly because Paul doesn't spend much time describing it. He will a bit in the weeks to come, but his strategy in Colossians is predominantly offensive rather than defensive. Rather than focus on the problem, he dwells on the solution.

Let's be honest. We all at some point question whether or not Jesus is worth what he asks of us. Or whether he really is all the ridiculously wonderful things we say we believe he is. Or if he is where we are most likely to find authentic life and love and peace. What I love most about Colossians is that Paul identifies the very best possible strategy for fighting these temptations. He retells the truth about Jesus.

We all think we know what the church needs. We're often tempted to think our church's greatest needs are financial or personnel-related or strategic. I don't doubt that some of these are legitimate. But none of them are what the church needs first and always and most. What our churches need most is not a bigger budget or better youth events or a new leader. We aren't dying for lack of management techniques or public relations strategies or more relevant ways of doing church. Our problems won't be solved by new seating arrangements or more programs or deeper teaching. What the church absolutely cannot live without is a clear vision of the one who claims us as his own. What we need most is simply to see Jesus.

Visibility

Chapter 8 – Colossians 1.15

When my wife was eight years old, her third grade math teacher noticed that while Beth did fine on homework assignments, she couldn't differentiate between numbers on the chalkboard. Obviously this concerned the teacher, so she encouraged Beth's mom to have her eyes checked. Sure enough, the doctor discovered, Beth needed glasses. Matter of fact, he said she'd probably needed them since before kindergarten.

Freshly bespectacled with frames about four times the size of her face, little Beth sat in awe the entire drive home as the world came alive all around her. Realizing for the first time that there were actual words on the signs lining the streets, she read every one aloud: "Circle K! Walmart! Main Street!"

When they finally arrived – Beth giddy with delight and her mom fighting back tears of guilt – she stepped out of the car and froze. With mouth open and bulging eyes locked in amazement on the trees in her front yard, she dramatically exclaimed, "Mom, there are leaves *on* the trees!"

Remember how we drew trees as little kids – those textureless green clouds perched atop a brown tube? She thought trees really looked like that. She didn't know leaves existed until they hit the ground. No pattern. No detail. No definition.

God is for many of us not unlike a leafless tree.

I doubt if anyone makes it through life without asking the question, "What is God like?" Identities, marriages, families, religions, even whole societies have developed based on shared answers to this question. Sadly, competing answers have wreaked chaos on the same.

I recently sat on an interfaith Q&A panel for a local organization. As the "evangelical Christianity" representative, I sat alongside a Muslim, a Buddhist, a Unitarian, and a Jewish rabbi.[8] We actually had a great time and all but one of us stayed on our best behavior. (No, I was not the naughty one.) However, I couldn't help but think about the fact that at least four of us have essentially invented an idea, given it the name "God" – or something vaguer but every bit as authoritative – and offered ourselves as its devotees.

I don't want to invent God. I want to discover God. I want to find God, or rather be found by him. I want to see God for who God really is. But how?

Do you ever feel this way? The irony in all this is that you and I were created to clarify precisely this confusion.

Imagine for a minute that there actually *is* life in some faraway galaxy. (Didn't expect me to go crazy sci-fi all of a sudden, did you?) They too have been created by God, of course, so they have some inkling of him. Internally they sense themselves drawn to God, but they don't know who he is. What would they do? Duh, they'd exercise their advanced intelligence to search the universe for clues God may have left about his identity and purposes. They come across this little marble called Earth, which is inhabited by funny-looking two-leggers named humans. Awhile back some Klingons mentioned a popular tradition that these folks were created "in God's image, in his likeness," and so provided the only known reliable clue about who God is.

So they decided to pay us a visit. By what are they greeted as they step off their ship? A drunk dude in a ditch, teenagers knife-fighting over what seem to be different colored costumes, and a man with loveless eyes handing money to a woman who appears not to have enjoyed his company.

---

[8] Yes, I am aware that this sounds like the beginning of a bad joke, especially when you consider where it took place: "So a Muslim, a Rabbi, a Unitarian, a Buddhist, and an evangelical walk into a Senior Center…" I'll let you write the rest.

And all this was before they found a television and caught an hour's worth of "world news."[9]

They should look at us and see God's mercy, but instead we show them injustice and exploitation of the weak. They should see God's provision, but instead we show them addiction. They should see kindness, but instead we show them abuse. They should see gentleness, but instead we show them rape. They should see patience, but instead we show them war.

As one scholar put it, "Humanity was designed to be the perfect vehicle for God's self-expression within his world."[10] But those created to clarify have only compounded confusion. Adding tragedy to irony, even we are not the kind of beings capable of seeing God as God actually is – at least not if we want to live to tell the story. At best we catch glimpses, no clearer in detail than a child finger-painting a forest.

But according to Paul, God has not left humanity in the dark. Paul opens his poem by clarifying something about Jesus, and in turn something about God: *He is the image of the invisible God* (Col 1.15a). Jesus is the way that God, who is invisible, makes himself visible. The God we cannot see "moves into our sphere of sense perception" in the life of Jesus.[11] The Great Optometrist has given us eyes to see. What corrective lenses do for trees, Jesus does for God.

Paul doesn't speak on his own here, but merely adds his voice to what the first Christians were saying left and right:

In the past God spoke to our ancestors through the prophets at many times and in various ways, but in these last days he has spoken to us by his Son, whom he appointed heir of all things, and through whom also he made the universe. The Son is the radiance of God's glory and the exact representation of his being, sustaining all things by his powerful word.

– Hebrews 1.1-3a

In the beginning was the Word, and the Word was with God, and the Word was God. He was with God in the beginning. No one has ever

---

[9] Major Ian Thomas, *The Indwelling Life of Christ* (Colorado Springs: Multnomah), 13-19.

[10] N. T. Wright, *Colossians* (Downers Grove: IVP Academic), 74.

[11] Marianne Meye Thompson, *Colossians & Philemon* (Grand Rapids: Eerdmans, 2005), 28.

seen God, but the one and only Son, who is himself God and is in closest relationship with the Father, has made him known.

– John 1.1-2, 18

Think about this for a second. Without Jesus, we'd still be sitting in a dark room straining to see by nothing more than the tiny sparks of a lighter that no longer works. Without Jesus, we'd have nothing but half-true, half-make-believe deities. Without Jesus, we would have no way of knowing God in grace and truth. Can I state the obvious? That would be really, really bad.

People in Paul's world certainly weren't at a loss for gods to choose from. One ancient playwright quipped that it was easier to trip over a god than a human. The gods were everywhere, including Colossae. The most famous god worshiped there and elsewhere was Zeus, who by conservative estimates forcefully impregnated two-dozen nonconsensual mortal women.

Also popular in Colossae was the goddess Demeter. One time Demeter got angry at a man for harming wood nymphs by cutting down the tree they lived within. She struck him with hunger so insatiable that he sold his own daughter into slavery to buy food. Eventually he started gnawing at his own flesh until he ate himself alive. Another local faith centered on the god Attis and goddess Cybele. All you had to do to become a leader in this group was castrate yourself and offer your genitals as a sacrifice.

We'd be stuck with gods like that. Or we'd be left to tribal deities, local gods invented to serve only the needs of our family, our business, our country, or our empire. We already talked about how Roman emperors like Augustus and his successors were granted divine or semi-divine status. We don't generally offer such cult-like devotion to our leaders, but question the ideals they stand for and you'll certainly incur something not unlike the wrath of gods. We may not know Mammon or Mars or Aphrodite by name, but their spirits linger. It's all very messy and depressing, really.

Good thing Jesus entered the business of making visible what we otherwise could never see.

Do you want to know how God responds to women caught in adultery?
Do you want to hear what God thinks of religion?
Do you want to see how God feels about poverty?

Do you want to know how God treats the people you hate?
Do you want to hear what God says to outcasts and sinners?
Do you want to see what God is doing about human suffering?

Do you want to know whom God blames for natural disasters?
Do you want to hear whom God considers the real enemy?
Do you want to see how God deals with illness and sorrow and death?

Do you want to know his gentleness?
Do you want to hear his judgment?
Do you want to see his grace?

Do you want to know? Do you want to hear? Do you want to see?

God has shown you who God is. God has revealed. God is The One Who Looks Like Jesus. Jesus is the image of The One Who Otherwise Cannot Be Seen.

Image
Chapter 9 – Colossians 1.15

When I was a child my grandmother told me the story of a man born with a crooked back who spent twelve hours a day staring at the statue of a man who stood straight and tall and true. His family and friends understood his strange behavior at first, but over time they became concerned that comparing himself to someone so magnificent would only send him into deeper depression over what he could never become.

But the man with the crooked back was not deterred. Twelve hours a day. Every day. Staring at the same statue of the same man with perfect posture. As you might have guessed if your grandmother told you similar stories, the shape of the staring man's back began to change. Slowly, even imperceptibly at first, each day he stood a fraction straighter and taller than before. Eventually – always just in time for me to go to bed – one could hardly tell the difference between the man and the model he so patiently and consistently sought to imitate.

Who are you staring at? What image defines the good life in your imagination?

I was thinking about this earlier today while buying clothes for my wife. I'm not very good at buying women's clothes, but Mothers Day will be here soon and she asked for some new pajamas. So there I am, hopelessly wandering through the women's section at our local department store, met in every direction by the eyes of some image telling my wife, my daughter, and all other female shoppers what they're supposed to look like (if only they'll buy this summer dress or those colorful camis, of course).

Then I come home and turn on the TV, only to be greeted by multiple versions of a cultural artifact so common we hardly even notice it anymore: the commercial. One of my long favorites has been the Mac vs. PC series pitting the almost accidentally cool semi-hipster against the frumpiest dude you know. Of course they're not actually selling product; they're selling image. Same goes for Nike, Disney, the NFL, and Taco Bell. I'm not saying the products are lame, I'm just saying that the products alone aren't what keep us coming back. And marketers know this. If they can somehow tap into our (typically subconscious) image of what makes for a good and happy life, then we'll buy whatever they're selling.

So let me ask again: Who are you staring at? The latest well-known CEO or computer guru? Today's favorite daytime talk show host or professional athlete? The proverbial PTA Mom? The prototypical #1 Dad? Each of us is hardwired to imitate. Even people who say they don't aim to be anyone but themselves are imitating all the other people who say the very same thing. We all pattern ourselves after some model, some ideal, some image.

Believe it or not, we still aren't ready to move beyond the first line of Paul's poem: *He is the image of the invisible God.* Yesterday we explored what this statement reveals about God. Today we're going to discover what it says about us.

Paul takes us back to the beginning of our story as told in the Bible's opening chapter. There we discover that we have been created *in God's image*.

> Then God said, "Let us make mankind in our image, in our likeness, so that they may rule over the fish in the sea and the birds in the sky, over the livestock and all the wild animals, and over all the creatures that move along the ground."
>
> So God created mankind in his own image,
> > in the image of God he created them;
> > male and female he created them.
>
> God blessed them and said to them, "Be fruitful and increase in number; fill the earth and subdue it. Rule over the fish in the sea and

the birds in the sky and over every living creature that moves on the ground. "

– Genesis 1.26-28

In ancient cultures only one person was said to be created "in the image of God," and that person was the king. To be made in God's image was to be charged with the task of mirroring the gods' heavenly kingdom above in one's earthly kingdom below. This explains why we see so much talk of *ruling over* the rest of God's good creation. This ancient mission has been democratized in the Bible, where we learn that together as a human family – male and female – we have been delegated to reflect God's loving rule toward one another and the non-human world. This is literally what we were made for, why we were put here in the first place.

Easier said than done, right?! Genesis's portrait of humanity's role inspires great good, but unfortunately these words have often been abused to support some of our worst and least God-like tendencies.

The good news is that Genesis wasn't meant to be the end but only the beginning. Much later, in Colossians, Paul opens the curtain a little wider and lets us in on more of the back-story. What did you notice about the way Genesis and Paul talk about God's image? Clearly the two are related, but did you catch the difference?

Genesis says we were made *in* the image of God. Colossians says Jesus *is* the image of God.

This means that when we look at Jesus, we see the template God used to create humanity. We see who we were always designed to become. From the beginning we were made to mirror the one we now know as Jesus Christ. He is the prototype, the portrait, the map. He is the model of authentic humanity. When we look at Jesus, we see the first genuinely *normal* human being.

Let that sink in for a minute. Have you ever wondered what God wants from you? What God wants for you? Who God made you to be? It's not just teenagers who lay awake at night and stare at the stars who wonder if they're reaching the reason they appeared, if they're becoming the person the heavens originally had in mind. God didn't create you to mirror the famous TV personality, the superb athlete, the model with the perfect body, or the cool guy wearing Chucks and spitting wit. God created you to look like Jesus. He is the image according to which you were dreamed up. He is your God-given destiny.

Now of course this doesn't mean that each of us ought to have become a renegade rabbi who died on a cross to save the world from sin. We're not talking about those kinds of things. We're talking about character, virtue, love. I think Dallas Willard explains this best: You were made to be and do whatever Jesus would be and do if he were you.[12] If he lived in your shoes and had your family, your friends, your enemies, your neighbors, your house, your dog, your clothes and your job. (Of course, there's always the chance he'd sell all your clothes and quit your job, but that's another story.)

You were fashioned to love God the way Jesus loved God, to trust God the way Jesus trusted him – up to and even through the point of losing everything. You were formed to see people the way Jesus saw them, to love people the way Jesus loved them – up to and even through the point of giving everything. You were designed with Jesus in mind.

Scholars and teachers through the first few centuries of Christian history devoted their blood, sweat, tears, and in some cases even their lives to protecting the orthodox doctrine of Jesus' full divinity and humanity. They taught us that Jesus is 100% human and 100% divine. We're not going to get into the details of how "theological math" works, but at least now we can understand why they cared so much. The question is basically whether or not Jesus answers our essential questions: Who is God? Who are we?

Over the past two chapters we've explored the essential starting point for discovering the answers – or rather, the *answer*. Do you want to know what God is like? Look at Jesus. Do you want to know how to live your life? Look at Jesus. What you need most is not a meditation program or counseling or self-actualization. What you need is not to dabble in Buddhism or to find the secret that unlocks the divine spirit within. Some of these things are probably demonic and others are helpful, but none of them are what you require above all else. What you need most is simply a clear vision of Jesus.

Jesus is the full and final revelation of who God is and who we were created to be. There is no reason to look anywhere else for the Divine, nor will we ever find another model that stands as straight and tall and true.

---

[12] Dallas Willard, *The Divine Conspiracy* (San Francisco: Harper Collins, 1998), 283.

Creation
Chapter 10 – Colossians 1.15-17

Everywhere you go and in everything you do, you deal with things.
Persons. Places. Properties. Ideas. Objects. Systems. Chairs. Tables. Magnets.
Nouns. Verbs. Prepositions. Outer space. Urban space. Cyberspace.
Basketball. Volleyball. Lacrosse. Tests. Cheerleading. Tae Kwon Do. Dust.
Carpet. Paper. Weights. Words. Hugs. Fists. Feasts. Ideals. Idols.

Life is literally full of things. Right now you're reading a book or an e-
reader or a mobile app, probably while relaxing on a couch or sitting at a
desk or lying in bed. Hopefully not while driving a car. Maybe you're
enjoying a glass of milk or a cup of coffee or a pot of tea. Perhaps you just
finished eating. Hopefully it was Italian. Most of you have arms and legs
and eyes and ears and fingers and toes. You have a brain too, and a heart,
lungs, reproductive organs, and a colon. I'd assume you're wearing clothes,
and maybe a necklace or a ring or a hat. Depending on your age and where
you live, you've probably spent more than a few years living in a home,
being raised by parents or caretakers, and matriculating through a school
system. Maybe you have a dog or a fish. Maybe you have a job or a dream.

What's more, you're thinking about something. Hopefully you're
focusing on Jesus and Paul and the book of Colossians, but that's probably
not enough to occupy your entire range of mental capacities. (Which is a
fancy way of saying, "This ain't the only thing in your head.") Maybe you're
having trouble concentrating on what I'm saying because you can't stop

thinking about a boy or a girl, a boss or an employee, a growing child or an aging parent, the car that needs fixing, the house that needs selling, the report that needs writing, the meal that needs cooking, or the kitchen that needs cleaning.

Life is so thing-y. We can't get away from it, nor do we typically want to, so we learn to navigate this world of things. Rather than ignore the kids, we raise them. Instead of piling up clothes, we do the laundry. Since we can't avoid time in the restroom, why not bring along some reading material?

Sometimes we stop to ask why, or where it all came from, or how it all fits together. We're certainly not the first to lay awake at night and wonder. But more often we just go about our business without giving most things a second thought.

When Paul says "creation," he's talking about all these things. And Paul has quite a bit to say about creation in his poem about Jesus. Today we'll explore what his ideas have to do with all these things, but first we need to clear away some cobwebs that may keep us from hearing Paul on his own terms. When it comes to creation, we modern folks typically focus on *process*. We want to know the process or method that unfolded from the beginning to the present. Ancient folks reflected on creation with every bit of the energy and intelligence that we do, but for the most part they asked different questions. Generally speaking, they focused on *purpose*. What is it all for? What holds it all together? I guess you could say their approach was more philosophical while ours is more scientific. Or to oversimplify a bit, we obsess over questions of *how*: How did creation begin? How did it get from there to here? But they meditated more on questions of *why* and even *who*: Who is responsible for existence and why are we all here?

With all this in mind, let's examine Colossians 1.15-17:

He is the image of the invisible God, firstborn over all creation, for in him all things were created – in the heavens and on earth, things visible and invisible, whether thrones or lordships or rulers or authorities. All things have been created through him and to him, and he is before all things and in him all things hold together.

Let's break this down into four statements Paul makes about Christ and creation.

First, Paul says Jesus is the *firstborn over all creation*. "Firstborn" isn't really the best translation, because in English it only means one thing – the kid we had first – while the Greek word has a broader range. But there's really not a better word, so it'll have to do. It can mean both priority in time and primacy of rank, and here Paul emphasizes the latter.[13] For instance, Israel was called God's "firstborn son" in Exodus 4.22; she was obviously not the actual first nation in terms of time, but nonetheless held a primary place because of her importance for God's mission. Similarly in Psalm 89.27, God promises to *appoint* the king "to be my firstborn, the most exalted of the kings of the earth." You can't appoint someone to have been born first, but you can appoint him to the throne that sits above all others. And that's what Paul says here about Jesus. Jesus enjoys pride of place as the highest-ranking officer in creation, the one who rules over its every inch.

Paul grounds that first claim in the second: *For all things have been created in* and *through him*. Christ was the means or instrument by which God created, as well as the sphere in whom creation takes place. What in the world does this mean? It means God did nothing creation-related apart from Christ. It's a bit like asking someone if they were present at the party of the century, and then finding out that (a) they threw the thing, (b) it took place at their house, and (c) they own the car that dropped you off. Creation is Christ's party, and everyone else arrived via his invitation and his transportation.

With the third, Paul jumps from origin to purpose: *All things were created to* or *for him*. Up to this point Paul has offered high praise, but nothing unheard of in ancient Judaism. Jewish writers and philosophers talked about "Wisdom" or "Word" being the instrument through which God made all things (like in Proverbs 8.23). Here, however, he ups the ante by affirming about Jesus that no Jew claimed about anything outside God himself. Jesus is not only the starting point, but also the *goal* of absolutely everything. "Christ" names something integral to the purpose of every substance and system, every note and niche, every this and that and those other things as well.

---

[13] Paul isn't just saying that Christ is the first among equals, as if he's at a higher place on the same level as everything else God made. Paul had plenty of words to use to make that point, but that isn't the point he wants to make. For details see Murray Harris, *Exegetical Guide to the Greek New Testament: Colossians and Philemon* (Nashville: B&H, 2010), 39-40.

Finally, Paul pulls everything tight by writing *in him all things hold together*. This might be the strangest statement of all, especially for us scientifically-inclined folks. One older scholar famously explained that the law of gravity is an expression of the mind of Christ.[14] That sounds awesome, but I'm not sure what in the world it means!

To get Paul's point, we need to understand some ideas floating around the ancient world. A few philosophers watched the world and noticed two principles at work: change and consistency. Everything is always morphing, but at the same time our world keeps ticking on as before. You may have noticed the same concept at work in your own life. Picture you on your first day of high school – goofy haircut, embarrassing clothes, the whole nine yards. That isn't the "you" we know and love today, but it was still 100% you, right? Now you see what they noticed: harmony and yet variety; difference and yet sameness.

Think of the cosmos like a tapestry. You can't find any discernable pattern when viewed from one side, but turn it over and everything has its place.[15] Ancient folks called that connecting thread *logos* or "reason," and many devoted their lives to falling in its line. Paul's vision goes one step further: Creation's glue is not a principle, an idea, or a virtue, but a person. Jesus is the thread weaving together the chaotic fabric of our universe.

Everything in our world was created in and through Jesus, and everything has been designed to serve his purposes. Nothing finds true meaning outside his rule, nor is anything properly wielded when taking orders from any kingdom other than his. He is our source and our sustenance, our plot and our resolution, our inauguration and our consummation. Without him existence would not exist. Apart from his ongoing nourishment everything would disintegrate into nothingness.

He is the who and the why behind everything you see. Actually, that isn't saying enough. He is the Who, the Where, the Why, the How, and the What For that is behind, in front of, around, and all the way through every large and little thing that does, has, or will ever come into being. (Say that ten times fast!) No wonder one person called him "the integrating center of reality" and another "the center and circumference" of all things.[16]

All this of the one we typically just call Jesus.

---

[14] J. B. Lightfoot, *The Epistles of St Paul: Colossians and Philemon* (London: Macmillan, 1875).

[15] Andrew Lincoln, "Colossians" *NIB*. Vol 11 (Nashville: Abingdon, 2000), 609.

[16] Thompson, 31; Sweet and Viola, 1.

Power

Chapter 11 – Colossians 1.16

Six-year-old Diane Disney asked her father a very important question, "Are you Walt Disney?"

"Of course, darling," he said. "Who did you *think* I was?"

"What I mean is . . . are you the *famous* Walt Disney who makes movies? Someone at school said you were."

He smiled and nodded. She blushed, held out a piece of paper, and asked for his autograph. He took out his fountain pen and happily dashed off his world famous signature.

"Oh, thank you, Daddy!" she gasped, and then skipped off into a world a bit larger than the one she inhabited five minutes before.[17]

You may be finding out for the first time that Jesus is more than you originally bargained for. You thought you were getting a meaningful spiritual experience or a fresh start or post-death access into heavenly bliss. Come to find out you now know the visible image of our invisible God and the template for authentic humanness, who also happens to be the one in, through, and for whom all things came into being. All this from a few lines about Christ and creation.

---

[17] *The Story of Walt Disney: Maker of Magical Worlds* (New York: Bantam Doubleday), 1.

It might be wise at this point to pause and ask why Paul talks so much about creation. The whole first half of his poem centers on Christ's relation to it. Why?

In the Old Testament we see countless examples of the same sort of argument. Why? Because God suffered no shortage of competition for people's faith and devotion. The surest way to tell who deserved to rule the world was by asking who put it here in the first place. If God created everything, then only God is worthy of our worship and love. To bow before anything else is to worship something *less powerful*, which is kind of dumb if you think about it. Paul follows the same logic in reference to Jesus.

We're almost ready to dive into the second half of Paul's poem, but first we need to explore what might be the weirdest line of all. I'll highlight the part I'm talking about below:

For in him all things were created –
in the heavens and on earth,
things visible and invisible,
whether thrones or dominions or rulers or authorities.
All things have been created through him and to him,
and he is before all things and in him all things hold together

Whether thrones or lordships or rulers or authorities catches my attention for a couple reasons. First, it is completely unnecessary.

Question: If you take away all things both in heaven and on earth, including everything you can see and everything you can't see, what do you have left?

Answer: Nothing! Yet Paul feels the need to add *whether thrones or lordships or rulers or authorities.*

It's like saying, "I love absolutely everything about you, and I love the color of your eyes." Apparently Paul never learned the word "implied" in vocabulary class.

Come to think of it, though, in some situations the extra detail makes perfect sense. Everyone dislikes something about the mirror, so what if the girl you love thinks she has really ugly eyes? I suggest that you very soon and often tell her that you love absolutely everything about her, and that you love the color of her eyes.

Details in question must be included to reinforce what we already know but have a hard time genuinely believing. (You might want to read that sentence again.) Could the "things" Paul singles out represent just such a necessary caveat? Let's examine the actual words and find out.

We all know what *thrones* are, and here throne speaks of the chair that symbolizes the influence of someone in a powerful position. Sort of like "White House," the position or office this represents will outlast any individual who lives there.

Dominions, which could also be translated "lordships," are realms ruled over by a person or group. The land we call "Switzerland" is the dominion of the Swiss government. The place you call "kitchen" may be the dominion of your mother or your father, depending on who's more gifted with the grub. They exercise "lordship" over these domains.

Rulers translates a word that can mean first in time ("beginning") or first in rank ("ruler"), and always refers to something or someone's superiority. Here we're talking about the person with the most influence and therefore the greatest capacity to tell everyone else how it is. More simply, the guy at the top.

Authorities refers to those with legitimate authority, such as a principal, parent, or policeman. They enjoy the ability to do or demand things based on their official position.

Two things stand out to me: (1) These terms seem loose and interchangeable, almost like saying someone is beautiful, stunning, gorgeous, and attractive. (2) Every item on this list refers to some form of power.

But what kind of power? Two basic answers have been offered. Some say that Paul is talking about personal spiritual beings, like what we typically call "angels" or "demons." Others suggest that Paul's "powers" are best understood as the systems or structures or institutions that govern human social life. Think about normal things like families, nations, religions, school systems, banks, universities, or department stores. All these are ways we organize our lives by giving certain kinds of power to a group that is bigger than any one individual. We sometimes personalize these things too, like when we talk about social or economic "forces" or sticking it to The Man.

We give these systems power, but then we often find ourselves enslaved to their rules. (Like when your boss fires you and blames Corporate, who blame the Shareholders, who blame the Market, which relies on the very people losing their jobs.)

Scholars spend hundreds of pages debating these options, and some of it is actually pretty fascinating. But today we'll keep things pretty simple. I'll tell you what I think, give you three quick reasons why, and then we can get on with it. I think Paul is talking about both. His terms encompass both "spiritual" powers and "social" or "political" forces. Here are my reasons:

1) *Paul's terms refer to both forms of power in other places in the New Testament.* Those sitting on "thrones" include God (Matthew 5.34), Satan (Revelation 2.13), the Apostles (Matthew 19.28), Jesus (Matthew 25.31), and earthly political rulers (Luke 1.52). "Rulers" is used of both human leaders (Luke 12.11; Titus 3.1) and spiritual powers (Ephesians 6.12; Jude 1.6), as is "authorities" (Romans 13.1; Luke 12.11; Ephesians 3.10, 6.12).

2) *In Paul's world, the two realms were not considered distinct but rather overlapping.* Folks in Paul's world believed that gods stood behind earthly rulers and authorities as well as the systems that kept society going. The spiritual and social/political were different sides of a single coin. Individual gods or angels were tasked with watching over particular cities or industries or families or nations. Everything on the "spiritual" level of reality impacted the "physical," and everything on the earthly level reflected events in the heavenly realms. Worshiping properly was seen as necessary to making sure the real world continued running smoothly.

3) *Paul specifically refers to things that are not only invisible and heavenly, but also visible and earthly.* Given how intentionally Paul includes *everything,* it seems unwise to limit his words to only half of the specific categories he mentions.

So Paul is talking about any and all spiritual-social forces that exert power over you and me.

All this brings us back to our first question: Why add this line in the first place? What led Paul to clarify that even the Powers That Be were created under, in, through, and for Jesus? Why was "all" not enough, especially when paired with "in heaven and earth, visible and invisible"?

Because there's always an exception, right? When you were reading the last chapter about Jesus being bigger and older and stronger than absolutely everything, did it not seem a little farfetched? I'm not even talking about the science of it all. I'm talking about the fact that Jesus just doesn't seem big enough to focalize and encompass everything. He's great with the "spiritual" or religious part of our lives, but can we really trust him to be the master and commander of *everything*?

Best we can tell, the Colossians were starting to wonder about the exceptions. As one author put it, "They believed that Christ was a true revelation of God with authority over *part of* human experience and conduct, but that other aspects of life must be controlled by other authorities with an equal claim to derive from God."[18] They started listening to folks who admitted Jesus was important but said to hedge your bets by getting on the good side of other Figures or Forces as well. Or that Jesus provided a decent start, but for a truly fulfilling religious experience you should tap into a few other sources of spiritual power too.

Either way, they were being drawn away from undiluted allegiance to Jesus. And Paul thought that was just silly.

Paul emphasizes Jesus' role in creation generally, and specifically in relation to every powerful force or figure in heaven or on earth, in order to communicate one truth: Nothing and no one in this or any other world is more powerful than Jesus. Not America or China or Al-Qaeda. Not Walmart or Nike or Penn State or Harper Collins. Not ghost-whisperers or dream-catchers or voodoo queens. Not Michael or Gabriel or whatever other angel you've been touched by. Not Incubus or Pazuzu or Satan himself.

Everything came into being through Jesus, was created for Jesus, and holds together in Jesus. Therefore, nothing is more powerful than Jesus. No one promises better, nor can anyone deliver more. No one else has the authority to ask for your unflinching obedience, nor does anyone's power ultimately deserve your fear.

If you don't think Jesus is that big, then Jesus is bigger than you think.

---

[18] G. B. Caird, *Paul's Letters From Prison* (Oxford University Press), 163.

Restart

Chapter 12 – Colossians 1.18

Let's say I barge into your cubicle tomorrow morning and excitedly inform you that as of last Saturday, new testimony has arrived from the edges of our solar system and confirmed that Pluto is, in fact, a planet after all. Since you look puzzled, I remind you that just a few years ago the scientific community ruled that Pluto is not, in fact, a planet but actually nothing more than a plutoid. Aside from wondering who in the world I am – and what in God's name is a plutoid – you notice that I seem genuinely thrilled not only to have discovered this truth but to have been given the opportunity to share it with you. The only problem is, you just as genuinely could not care less.

What do you say? You could go the kind route: That's nice. Exciting. Woooowwww. Or you could skip the pleasantries and shoo me away with how you really feel: So what? What difference does it make? Who cares? (Or even, What exactly is wrong with you?)

What if what we talked about over the last two chapters is true? What if everything in our world really has been created through, in and for Christ? What if he holds it all together and enjoys the honor of being its only legitimate Lord?

That's nice. Exciting. Woooowwww.

We aren't much for theory. We don't just want the facts; we want the *relevant* facts. We are action-oriented, practical people. We want to get to work. Tell me what I need to know to do *this*, and I'm good. Save the other stuff for a classroom. I live in the real world and in the real world that kind of trivial information only slows people down.

If you want to talk to me about God, tell me what God is doing about the crap I'm dealing with. So what if my forklift was designed in and for Jesus? Tell me how I can work fewer hours and still keep a roof over my family. Who cares if Christ invented cast iron? Show me where I can get the money for a new skillet.

Matter of fact, the claim that everything was created in and for Jesus is not only vague and seemingly irrelevant. It's also incriminating. Assuming for the moment that it's true, how can we not conclude that Jesus has done a poor job of managing what he made? Even if we grant "free will" and don't directly blame him for genocide, poverty, or the divorce rate, how are we supposed to worship Jesus if this is the best he can do? The Titanic was certainly an impressive ship except for the fact that it sank. It's the sinking part we remember. Surely a poem about the Titanic's greatness is only halfway done if it hasn't addressed that not-so-minor detail.

So by this point Paul has two strikes against him. First, he's sharing information that seems disconnected from our daily lives. That's cool about Jesus revealing God's identity and human destiny and all, but why talk about ideals when we're stuck in a world that so obviously fails to measure up. If Jesus hasn't done anything to fix *this* world – this starving child and that abused woman and those depressed folks on the corner lot with all the toys – then what's the point? Second, he's making claims that seem ridiculous. If Jesus is more powerful than any force in the universe, then why is the nightly news so depressing?

What is God's solution to the real world we live in? That's the code we want cracked. Paul kicks off the second half of his poem with the key: resurrection.

Here is what he actually writes in Colossians 1.18:

He is the founder, firstborn from among the dead, so that in everything he might enjoy supremacy.

Paul says Jesus is literally the "first" or "beginning," which in this context basically means he started something new. Think Bill Gates or James

Naismith or Colonel Sanders, guys who started a new restaurant or sport or industry. These people are entrepreneurs or founders.

The next line defines what Jesus founded: *firstborn from among the dead.* Clearly Paul is talking about resurrection, but to get what he's saying I have a question for you.

If you had the necessary power and resources, how would you save the world? Would you assemble the wisest people alive, boil all their wisdom down to one or two lessons, and then build "aliens" to come from outer space and teach humans the secret to peaceful living? Actually that sounds expensive, and thanks to every other action film since 1985, most people would assume aliens are hostile and probably try to blow them up before learning the secret.

Maybe you could just send a mass email. Come to think of it, I'm pretty sure my cousin's aunt's mother-in-law already forwarded me that email. If that was legit and you were behind it, sorry but I don't read forwards. You'll have to heal the world without me.

Don't give up though. You have other options. You could go the science route. Concoct some tasteless, colorless liquid that reduces anxiety and causes people to think positively. Then subtly insert it into the water supply, and stand back to watch kindness take over. Then again, spreading love through unsolicited drug-induced personality alteration seems a little – what's the word? – hypocritical.

One popular solution is to separate the good people from the bad people, destroy the bad, and let the good folks naturally spread goodness through future generations. God actually tried this once with a guy named Noah. But if it didn't work well for God – and it didn't, unless getting drunk and waking up naked and angry is considered "spreading goodness" – we probably won't fare much better.

Not as easy as it sounds, eh? God's answers to questions like this can be kind of long – my Bible has 1189 chapters, and all but the first two show God saving the world – so we'll summarize. Today and tomorrow we'll explore God's answer by unpacking two long "r" words. First up is resurrection. God's solution for fixing this world is to establish a new one within the shell of the old.

After the Noah experiment, God set his mission in motion with the calling of Abraham. God came to Abraham, who at the time had no children, and promised that (a) he would have lots of kiddos and (b) his kiddos and their kiddos would be God's tool for saving the rest of the world. God swore to Abraham that come what may, this is how the world would be redeemed. And with this step, God introduced his basic strategy: Start small with this one group of people, teach them to embody the wise life, and then turn them loose to infiltrate human society from the inside. God starts small and works from within.

But chronically sick people can't make others well, and Abraham's family was infected with the same sin virus as everyone else. It's like when your Outlook freezes so you open Firefox to troubleshoot. Then Firefox freezes so you try Chrome, but that doesn't work either. The problem isn't one program but the system as a whole. Eventually you have to restart the computer. Resurrection is kind of like restarting your computer. You're not getting a different one or changing how the thing works, you're starting the same process over again but with confidence in a better outcome.

The people of Israel expected God to hit restart by defeating her enemies and resurrecting all Israelites from the dead. They would usher in a golden age of justice and peace as the founders of God's new world, and their holiness would spread outward to reach earth's end.

They were half right. God did hit restart, only not by raising everyone at once. God restarted with Jesus. God raising Jesus signals the *beginning* of a whole new world – a "new creation" untouched by sin and unthreatened by death. A world without slave traders or economic injustice or child abuse. A world where people will have their own land to work and families to love. A world where the metal from swords and machine guns will be recast into tools that serve life rather than taking it. A world where wolves will lie down alongside lambs without lambs becoming dinner.

This world is God's answer to every pain and struggle and sin you're dealing with right now. It is not fully here, of course, but it is on the way. Matter of fact, it is alive in you, but that's something we'll talk about in a couple weeks. For now Paul just wants us to know that it has begun. And not just that it has begun, but that it began in Jesus.

Reconciliation
Chapter 13 – Colossians 1.19-23

Sometimes it takes time to realize you've become part of something bigger than yourself. Sports do the trick for many kids. You practice for hours on jump shots, free throws, crossovers, spin moves, chest passes, and defensive stances. At first you're doing everything you can to become the best possible basketball player in general. But as you grow, based on your size and skill set, coaches identify your position: guard, forward, etc. The move is subtle but significant because it changes your approach to the game. You are no longer merely a basketball player. You now have a specific role as one member of a team. You practice even harder to get even better, but it's no longer just about you. It's about the team, or even the game as a whole.

For others it's learning to care less about a career and more about a company. For me it was getting married and having kids. For you it may have been volunteering for the PTA, serving on city council, or helping start a new church.

But for whatever reasons, faith seems to be the last place we abandon our personal thrones.

I want to ask you a question, and I want you to take a minute and really think about it: Why did you become a follower of Jesus?

Some of us were basically born into this. Others came along later because we had a moving experience of being loved by God, or because we got tired of fighting an addiction or depression on our own, or because we didn't want to go to hell. We came to Jesus because he promised us the very best life possible and we liked his offer better than the alternatives.

I'm not saying this is bad. It strikes me as no worse than a future point guard working on post moves because she doesn't yet understand the bigger picture. But sooner or later you need to realize that God's mission is not primarily about you. It's not about fixing your life, your career, your family, or even your eternity. God's mission includes all of these healings in crucial ways, but if we boil it down to any of them then we deform salvation into a me-centered affair.

It would be like if Batman made the entire epic entirely about his own inner healing or self-actualization. Of course part of the story is Bruce Wayne discovering his own identity and calling, but this subplot fits within the larger story of saving his beloved city.

Yesterday, Paul clarified God's grand plan for saving Gotham: inaugurate a new regime under the nose of those currently in power. Today Paul helps us envision not only God's strategy but especially his end game. We're talking about what God is trying to *do* on the most fundamental level. Here Paul sums up the goal of God's mission in one word: reconciliation.

Let's split today's text in half. Here's part one:

For in him all the Fullness was pleased to permanently dwell, and through him to reconcile all things to him – making peace through the blood of his cross – whether things on earth or things in the heavens.

– Colossians 1.19-20

Finally Paul takes his head out of the clouds long enough to realize that all is not well down here! Up to this point in the poem, Paul seems almost blind to the fact that the world is a jacked-up place. But here he subtly admits just this. Think about it: If something needs to be reconciled, then what is it currently? Separated. Hostile. Alienated. Out of whack.

Everything is estranged from its intended purpose. Angels become demons. Heroes become demi-gods. Good governments become evil regimes. Parents don't always love their kids, and kids don't always obey their parents. Precious metals are turned into tools of death rather than instruments of life.

Paul admits what we all know: Jesus may be the world's rightful ruler, but apparently some folks didn't get that memo. The world is out of sorts.

But he also confirms what we hope for: God is putting everything back together again, restoring everything to its intended place.

God's plan is not to destroy the world. God's plan is to save it. All of it. Everything from metals to mountains to mice (and I guess by default cats too, since mice will need someone to play with). The new world God is birthing will one day come in fullness and we will have seen the last of sickness, tears, violence, divorce, poverty, heartache, and death. It will be everything great about our world made even better, minus everything destructive.

How? By the peacemaking cross of Christ, of course.

And with that, Paul's poem comes to a close.

It's like the end of the second movie in what will obviously be a trilogy. The story doesn't really stop but just kind of pauses, the credits roll, the lights come on, and the entire theater thinks, "Really? That's all we get to see? You're stopping *there*?"

Thankfully, later on in this letter Paul will explain what this means. More immediately, if we wait through the credits we'll get an extra scene that moves the story a bit further along. Paul follows his poem with an appendix of sorts, still on the theme of reconciliation:

> *You too were once alienated, hostile in thought because of your evil deeds, but now he reconciled you in Christ's fleshly body through death, to present you holy and blameless and innocent in his sight, if indeed you continue in the faith, having been solidly established and firmly built, and don't get dislodged from the hope of the gospel you've heard. This gospel has been preached in all creation under heaven, and I, Paul, became its servant.*
>
> – Colossians 1.21-23

If everything needs to be reconciled, then so do we. We, too, are alienated. Paul uses this word "alienated" in another place talking about husbands and wives who are separated. They no longer live under the same roof, a geographical distance symbolizing the deeper rupture that has become their story. The future hangs in the balance: either this separation will become permanent in the tragedy of a love completely lost. Or they will be reconciled.

We are a broken people, alienated not only from God but from the role we were designed to play in his script for the universe. Paul paints our brokenness as a partnership between our thoughts and our behavior. God is not against us, but we are *hostile* toward him *in thought*. The way our mind works – how we process information and experiences – has settled into a pattern that not only rejects God but runs defiantly in the opposite direction. We're like a toddler who stares at mom throughout the act of disobedience as if to say, "You see this? Yeah, that's right. I have my own will and I'm exercising it." Or more hideously, a teenager who gives his father the finger before driving off in dad's car toward all manner of destructive activity.

Paul sees interdependence in the relation between our thinkings and our doings. Does our mind turn away from God and take our actions with it, or do we first disobey and our brain catches up to our rebellion? Yes.

We are completely out of whack. And the net effect is that the entire world suffers our foolishness. We're not just low-level employees, whom you can fire and replace with anyone else. We're store managers, the ones brought in to establish and maintain a well-functioning department or grocery or convenient store.

If God wants to put the world back together, God has to put us back together first. And this is precisely what the Jesus restart is all about. God sent in a new store manager – not to replace us but to restore harmony and show the rest of us how best to do our job.

But modeling alone isn't enough. The future needs fixing, but what about the past? We racked up a boatload of red during our days in charge, not to mention the legal messes. That debt's got to be paid; justice must be served. Which is why *he reconciled you in Christ's fleshly body through death, to present you holy and blameless and innocent in his sight,* even when we were disgusting and liable and deserving of death.

Do you understand what this means? Because of Christ's death on the cross, there is now no reason for you to feel out of place in God's presence, or to fear the day when you will find yourself there. You have been bathed in God's grace through the substitutionary death of Jesus. He died the death you deserved. You are now like a person brought before a judge or king to be sentenced, only to find out that even in casual gossip no one says a word against you. You are holy. You are blameless. You are innocent.

If indeed you continue in the faith, having been solidly established and firmly built, and don't get dislodged from the hope of the gospel you've heard.

Everything
Chapter 14 – Colossians 1.15-20

It is difficult to comprehend how small I am.

Recently I found a surprisingly helpful pair of allies in the National Football League and a scholar named Peter Berger.

Despite its violent nature and potential danger to the brains and bodies of those who play it best, football has supplanted baseball as the most popular sport in America. The NFL is the ninety-year-old, highly televised, multi-billion dollar industry that currently serves as the highest level of professional football in the world. You can love the league or hate it, but at least for the moment you know what it is.

On the other hand, Peter Berger is a brilliant and uber-heady sociologist, no doubt a much less public profession than NFL quarterback or commissioner, but every bit as potentially influential. He's probably most famous for co-authoring a humbling book called *The Social Construction of Reality*, which most folks have never heard of. Don't worry, all this means is that you're less nerdy than people like me.

A while back Berger wrote a column exploring the question of whether God cares about the outcome of certain NFL football games.[19] Sometimes

---

[19] Peter Berger, "Is God Interested in the Denver Broncos?" http://blogs.the-american-interest.com/berger/2012/03/07/is-god-interested-in-the-denver-broncos. Accessed 4/15/2012.

Jesus-loving players make near-miraculous plays that change the outcome of games, if not entire seasons. Are we seeing God at work?

I began the column expecting Berger to openly mock every semi-religious football fan for screaming, "Heaven yes, he did!!!!! Why? Because *GOD IS A BRONCOS FAN!*" Stuffy academics can be hilarious when ripping apart commoners like you and me, so I couldn't wait to hear what he had in store for football fanatics. But Berger's answer surprised me.

He first talks about an old man he once knew who often lost his keys. And whenever the keys couldn't be located, he and his wife would get on their knees and pray for help to find them. At the time Berger saw this as silly and absurd, often thinking about how God would more likely respond to legit concerns like world peace, the fate of nations, and food for the hungry. Who cares about lost keys when whole generations hang in the balance between poverty and peace?

But as he learned more about the God he said he believed in, he realized the equal *in*significance of both (technically speaking).

> If the creator of the universe, with its inconceivably vast and mysterious myriad of galaxies, pays attention at all to the affairs of beings on a small planet in a minor solar system—then *all these affairs should seem equally trivial to him*—the fate of a nation as little, or as much, as a set of lost car keys.

In other words, he continues, of course God cares about the outcome of NFL games, one way or another. Who but God knows the impact wins or losses might have on the world? If God doesn't care about them, then it makes no logical sense to say he cares about anything on our speck of a planet. He cares, not because football isn't trivial, but because in one sense the rest of our lives are too.

Technically, I am not important at all. God loves me fiercely, but only because of who God is. The human race certainly plays an important part in the world's story. But in the grand scheme, you and I are little more than nothing. It is actually difficult to grasp how diminutive we are.

In stark contrast, it is difficult to fathom how large Jesus is. This one God-Man integrates, well, everything.

You getting sick of that word yet? Everything. I've probably used it over a dozen times in the past few chapters. But don't blame me, I'm just trying to follow Paul's example. Let's lay out his poem in full, highlighting its primary recurring theme:

He is the image of the invisible God,
  *firstborn over **all creation**,*
    *for in him **all things** were created –*
      in the heavens and on earth,
      things visible and invisible,
      whether thrones or lordships or rulers or authorities.
  ***All things** have been created through him and to him,*

  *and he is before **all things***
    *and in him **all things** hold together;*
  and he is the head of the body, the church.

He is the founder,
  firstborn from among the dead,
    *so that in **everything** he might enjoy supremacy,*
    *for in him **all the Fullness** was pleased to permanently dwell,*
    *and through him to reconcile **all things** to him –*
      making peace through the blood of his cross –
      whether things on earth or things in the heavens.

See what I mean?! *All creation, everything, all the Fullness,* and in case you missed the point, five repetitions of *all things*.

But it's not just Paul's vocabulary that reveals Jesus as everything. The poem's overall structure makes the same point. Remember how I said we were going to examine the individual trees first, and then we'd back up and look at the whole forest? The individual trees have not disappointed. We've learned that only Jesus renders visible the God we cannot see, and that Jesus is the template we are patterned after and destined to become. We've seen Jesus as the glue that holds all things together and the rightful king of all things, since all things – even the most powerful – have been created in, through, and for him. Not only this, but the crucified Christ stands as the fountainhead of the river called resurrection that leads to the ocean named new creation. In him all things have been shown the way to healing and restoration, ourselves included, provided we stay the course.

We're finally ready to zoom out, almost like enjoying a helicopter tour of a forest trail we just finished hiking. And from up here we notice that these trees do fit together to form an intentional pattern. Paul's poem is broken into two main stanzas, with one mini-section in the middle that literally *holds* it all *together*.

Do you see how the two main parts parallel each other? Both begin with a statement about who Jesus is (*image* and *founder*), followed by a line featuring the word *firstborn*. Then the rest of both verses follows the same outline organized around the prepositions *in*, *through*, and *to*.

So they're similar, but obviously not the same. Each focuses on a different theme: creation first, and then reconciliation.

Quick question: What do you do all day? Are you a banker? A bartender? A football coach? A full-time mom? Whatever you do, chances are you can boil down your "job" to one or two primary, big picture tasks. Protecting money and making investments. Mixing drinks and monitoring drinkers. Offense and defense. Keeping kids alive and healthy today, and preparing them for tomorrow.

In a sense the same is true of God. His entire mission can be simplified into two functions: making the world and then repairing what it has become. Shaping and saving. Hatching and healing. Forming and fixing. Creating and reconciling.

Jesus plays an unparalleled and irreplaceable role in God's work of both creation and reconciliation. Jesus stands front and center in all divine activity. God does nothing apart from him. Jesus means everything for literally everything.

I realize this sounds a bit like what you said to your girlfriend or boyfriend when you were sixteen. Not the divine activity part, but the whole "You mean *everything* to me" bit. Except now we're adults and hormones don't (err, shouldn't) have the same reality-blinding effect on us that they did then. There is kind of a lesson here actually: We grow beyond many things, typically including our adolescent loves, but we never outgrow Jesus.

How can we? You may be big or smart or tough or pretty, but compared to Jesus you're basically an electron, which is part of an atom, which is part of a molecule, which is typically too small for our eyes to see. He, on the other hand, is the image of the invisible God and the forerunner of new creation, firstborn over both womb and grave, the one in, through, and for whom we were both made and remade – and not only us, but the entire universe. He is the context in which we grow as well as the energy behind growth itself. He is the one who made us. He is the one who saves us. He is more than enough for more than tiny little you or me. He is, in a word, everything.

And if Jesus plus nothing equals everything, what else do you need?

VISION

moreJESUS part 3 – CONFIDENCE

Confidence can be dangerous. One time a job applicant was asked about his primary strengths and weaknesses.

"Well," he began, "my main weakness would definitely be my issues with reality – telling what's real from what's not."

"Okay," said the interviewer. "And what are your strengths?"

"I'm Batman."[20]

Confidence has the potential to blind us from reality. Someone once said confidence is the feeling you have before you understand the situation. Do you think that's true? More specifically, do you think that's true about the Christian faith?

When it comes to the question of confidence and Jesus, you really only have four options:

(1) Jesus is false but you believe him confidently.

(2) Jesus is false and you don't believe him confidently.

(3) Jesus is true but you don't believe him confidently.

(4) Jesus is true and you believe him confidently.

Everything hangs on whether Jesus is authentically true. If he isn't who he says he is – if he isn't who I'm claiming he is in this book – then you would be foolish to believe in him confidently. If this is the case, then Jesus is definitely *not* all you need. In that case, if you want to live a full life and grow as a human being then you'd better be looking elsewhere.

On the other hand, if Jesus is who Christianity says he is, then you'd be silly not to confidently believe in him – in his glory, in his goodness, in his complete sufficiency for everything you need.

What else do you need? That is the question we're left with as we move to the third part of Paul's letter.

Remember that Paul wants us to walk away from this letter convinced that there is no legit reason to give our attention, devotion, allegiance, worship, or faith to anyone or anything other than Jesus. He plants his feet firmly in number (4) above: Jesus is true and you should believe in him confidently. Paul wants us to leave with no lingering suspicion that Jesus

---

[20] Readers Digest. http://www.rd.com/laughs/strengths-and-weaknesses-joke. Accessed 7/31/12.

needs to be added to, improved upon, accessorized, or augmented in any way. We don't need dream-catchers. We don't need horoscopes. We don't need angels. We don't need our candidate to get elected, our party to maintain majority, or our nation to last forever. We don't need spiritual secrets or mind-blowing visions. We don't need extra-terrestrial assistance or ritual pathways.

All we require is more of what God has already revealed. All we need is more of what we've already been given. All we need is more Jesus. Confidence in him is not dangerous, because he is everything we hope for and more. At least that's what Paul thinks. He offers a summary statement – both for this section and for the letter as a whole – in Colossians 2.5-6:

> *Therefore, just as you received Christ Jesus as Lord, continue walking in him, having been rooted and now being built up in him and being confirmed in the faith just as you were taught, overflowing with thanksgiving.*

By this time you recognize what he's saying: You don't need to go anywhere else. You just need to keep walking in the same direction – toward Jesus.

But Paul realizes that we aren't going to agree without a fight. We aren't idiots, and we aren't about to settle for cheap stale chocolate if someone down the street is swimming in Ghirardelli. We live in a virtual spiritual marketplace with as many religious alternatives as restaurant options. As well-trained consumers, we're not stupid enough to go to the same place every time we eat out. Which is fine when it comes to food. There's nothing wrong with eating Italian one week, Mexican the second, and sushi the third. The problem occurs when we bring this consumer mentality to matters of faith. Our consumer mentality paralyzes us from the kind of commitment Jesus calls for – the kind of commitment that alone would provide the foundation for the spiritual growth we crave and need.

As I've mentioned before, Paul's world wasn't much different. So in this next section he speaks to both worlds at once as he again sets out to prove his case for the uniqueness and adequacy of Jesus. His arguments are at once poetic, beautiful, confusing, pretentious, and in some cases just plain weird.

One more thought before we get to the text. Part of what may make Paul's case seem odd to us is that we tend to evaluate our spirituality by looking inward. Even as followers of Jesus, when we want to measure "how we're doing" in our faith journey, we examine things like our own habits or feelings or ways in which we're better today than we were last year. These can all be good and helpful in their proper context, but none of them should be primary. Paul does not point primarily inward toward how we feel like our life is going, or outward to what the world thinks of us. Instead he points upward to what Jesus has accomplished on our behalf. When we evaluate whether our faith deserves our confidence, the primary test is not ourselves. It is Jesus.

Apostle
Chapter 15 – Colossians 1.24–2.5

Have you ever noticed how often Paul talks about himself? In almost every letter he includes at least one biographical section. Sometimes he's just updating his friends on travel plans, logistics, that sort of thing. But much of the time he's defending himself and his style of ministry. Why?

The answer is actually pretty simple. Paul lived in a world where lots of people took it upon themselves to become teachers of humanity and educate everyone else on the truths of life in our universe. (Sound familiar?) Because of this, philosophers and educators would often lay down criteria for why a teacher should be taken seriously. Aristotle famously demanded that we see three things before we trust someone enough to take their advice. The first was *logos*, which basically involves making good sense. If someone comes around claiming that the secret to life is drinking battery acid (or the ancient equivalent), then they are obviously not a person to be taken seriously. Or if a teacher constantly contradicts their own teaching, they are not to be trusted. Aristotle's second requirement was *pathos*. This could mean emotion or passion. Basically, boring teachers shouldn't expect to win much of a hearing. If even you don't seem to believe what you're saying, then we're not going to either. The third requirement was *ethos*, and that's the one that will help us understand why Paul talks about himself so much. *Ethos* refers to the quality of the person doing the teaching. Do they have character and integrity? Do they practice what they preach? Do they truly want to help as opposed to just trying to make money or gather a crowd or make a name for themselves? If someone makes good sense (*logos*) and delivers their message in a compelling fashion (*pathos*) but doesn't live a respectable and selfless life (*ethos*), then many people in the ancient world would simply tune them out. And rightly so.

We wisely think the same way, of course, even if we might not line out the reasons so systematically. We want to know that the people we're listening to are trustworthy. We are naturally suspicious of infomercials and TV preachers and people who come to our door trying to sell us the latest and greatest vacuum cleaner or home security system.

So why listen to Paul? How does his *ethos* measure up? Maybe you've wondered why we base our lives on the teachings of a bunch of guys who lived two thousand years ago. Paul assumes you will, so it's not something to be ashamed about. It's actually a good thing, because it shows that you take your faith seriously and really try to think things through. Unfortunately Jesus himself never wrote a book. In the only record we have of Jesus writing something down, he was basically finger painting in the sand and no one even shared what he wrote. The Bible was written by prophets and apostles, Paul among them. But why should we listen to them? Why should we listen to him? With this in mind, let's explore Colossians 1.24-2.5.

> *Now I rejoice in suffering on your behalf, and I fill up in my flesh what is lacking of Christ's afflictions on behalf of his body, which is the church, of which I became a servant according to the commission God gave me: to fill up the word of God for you, the mystery which was hidden from past ages and generations, but now has been made visible to those set apart. To them God chose to make known the richness of the glory of this mystery among the Gentiles, which is Christ in you, the hope of glory. He is the one we publicly proclaim, admonishing everyone and teaching everyone in all wisdom, so that we might present everyone mature in Christ. To this end I labor intensely, striving with all his energy which powerfully energizes me.*
>
> *I want you to know how intensely I have struggled for you and those in Laodicea – for all those I haven't met in person – that their hearts might be encouraged, having been woven together in love. I want them to come to all fullness of the full assurance of understanding and knowledge of the*

mystery of God, which is Christ, in whom are hidden all the treasures of wisdom and knowledge. I tell you this so that none of you might be deceived by ideas that sound good on the surface. For I may be absent in flesh, but I am with you in Spirit, rejoicing and seeing your orderliness and the stability of your faith in Christ.

You may or may not have noticed, but this passage has a very purposeful underlying structure. (Actually, if you did notice, that's incredible and you have a future in literary analysis!) Paul uses a common ancient poem pattern called a "chiasm" that operates like a sideways V. For a very simple (and cheesy) example, consider the following sentences: *My Love, in my eyes you have no equal. Those who know you call me lucky. You are godly, beautiful, and strong. How fitting it is when others praise you. No other woman compares to you.*

Now let me show you the underlying organization of these same sentences:

> My Love, in my eyes you have no equal.
>> Those who know you call me lucky.
>>> You are godly, beautiful, and strong.
>> How fitting it is when others praise you.
> No other woman compares to you.

Notice how the first line fits with the last, both speaking of how I think my wife is second to none. And the second line fits with the second to last, both of which refer to other people's equally high opinion of her. Then there's an extra line in the middle. The idea is to emphasize the point in the middle. In my example this is where I reveal the basis for everyone's high opinion of My Love. Chiastic meter may seem weird and complicated, but people will say the same things about our poetry and music in a couple thousand years! Anyhow, let's take a bird's eye view of Colossians 1.24–2.5 with this grid in mind:

> Paul rejoices in suffering for them (1.24)
>> Paul reveals the mystery and its riches with wisdom (1.25-28)
>>> Paul's hard work and struggles (1.29-2.1)
>> Paul clarifies the mystery and its treasures of wisdom (2.2-3)
> Paul rejoices in their maturity and progress (2.5)

Notice what stands in the middle: Paul's hard work and struggles. Paul's point is simple: I've taken my share of lumps for what I'm telling you about Jesus. I've exhausted myself to get this done. I've been pressured and beaten and left for dead. I've suffered.

So far as I can tell, Paul is making three points here: (1) His labor and sufferings are a continuation of the sufferings of Christ. Jesus suffered to save us, and Paul suffered to bring us the good news that Jesus suffered to save us. (2) He is so convinced of what he's teaching that he'll gladly give his life so that more people might come to see that what he's saying about Jesus is true. (3) He isn't in this for himself, so you can at least trust that he's sincere. He's happy to hurt if his pain somehow serves others. That's how much Jesus means to him. That's how much we mean to him.

Paul wasn't just caught up in the moment. He meant every word, and he would later be given a chance to make the ultimate sacrifice. In the year AD 68, Paul demonstrated just how far he would go for the sake of Jesus, and for our sake so we could come to know Jesus. During his second trip to Rome, Paul was thrown into a prison surrounded by human filth in a room not even tall enough to stand in. From there he was marched across the center of Rome to a place of execution, where some unnamed Roman solider chopped off his head. And just like that the world lost one of its finest men.

And Paul was hardly alone. Of Jesus' original Twelve Apostles, only John died a natural death. The rest became martyrs, which means they died because of their commitment to Jesus. Peter was killed in Rome around the same time as Paul. In mockery of Jesus, the Roman soldiers crucified Peter too. But Peter didn't consider himself worthy of dying the same way as his Lord, so he asked to be crucified upside down. Philip, Thaddeus, Andrew, and Simon the Zealot were also crucified. Bartholomew was too, but not until after his skin was flayed. James and Matthias were both beheaded. James son of Alpheus was either stoned or thrown off the Temple, and his attackers finished the job by beating him with clubs. Matthew was stabbed to death. Thomas was speared and then thrown into an oven.

These men were not showboats, opportunists, liars, or crooks. Our faith is built on the backs of leaders worth trusting. Some may say the world needs heroes, and these men certainly qualify. But they would say the world already has its hero. The apostles lived and died as they did for one reason. They believed to their core that Jesus was worth it.

Resolution

Chapter 16 – Colossians 1.24–2.5

My friends in the entertainment industry tell me that insiders have a term for shows like CSI and Law & Order. They call them "bedtime stories." Their defining characteristic is that you can discover a problem, experience the need for closure, and live to see resolution in only sixty minutes. It's no accident they often air during the hour or two before most people hit the sack. These bedtime stories subtly bring good news of hope that even in a chaotic world where we can't always expect happy endings, we can at least expect that eventually mysteries will be solved, bad guys will be brought to justice, and we can all rest peacefully. Like children we crave resolution because, simply put, stories need endings.

The Old Testament is a story without an ending.

It's a magnificent and true story, to be sure. But it's not over when it ends. We can't yet go to bed, or at least we can't sleep peacefully. Why? Because there are too many unresolved issues, too many loose ends, too many undotted i's and uncrossed t's.

The big resolution question is obvious: When will God finish what he started? The problem that began with Adam was supposed to be solved by Abraham's family. God chose a people and promised that they would live forever in a land flowing with milk and honey. He promised to personally dwell in their midst. He promised that even after centuries of failure, the glory would return and bring with it a reign of life and love and peace. But he hadn't done it yet. To make matters worse, no one really knew how he would. Had God given up? Had he turned against his people? Would he come himself? Would he send someone else – a teacher perhaps, or a king? Would his appearance bring grace or judgment to his people? Would it bring both?

And what about everyone else? The whole world was supposed to be blessed and instructed and healed by the chosen ones. What will happen to the rest of us "Gentiles"? What will happen to those who ignored God's people, or worse, who killed them and destroyed their land? Will they be punished? Will they be forgiven? How will they come to know about the True God, the God of Israel, the Creator and Judge of all the earth?

These weren't just theoretical questions for God's people back in the day, because they directly led to a third set of questions: What do we do in the meantime? What does it look like for us to be faithful to the Law we hold so dear? How can we apply all the "wisdom" we've received from those who've gone before? Are we supposed to settle in, compromise, and make the best of a difficult situation? Are we supposed to move to the desert and wait for God to judge the ungodly and start over with us? Maybe God is waiting on us. Maybe God wants us to take the first move and fight like so many of the Old Testament heroes. Maybe we need to start a revolution against our enemies – however improbable our odds may seem – and *then* God will act on our behalf. Or could the problem be all the sinners and half-hearts among us? Should we separate ourselves from all those ungodly people so God will finally be pleased enough to act?

We shouldn't be surprised that many first century Jews lived on edge. It's no accident that on more than a few occasions, some young rebel would gather a band of brothers and attempt revolution. Their story needed an ending and they were quite willing to provide one.

Paul knew this story well, and it consumed his energies from a young age. Before meeting Jesus, Paul knew perfectly well how to answer the resolution questions, or so he thought. He put in with those who believed the world was still a mess because God's people had compromised. The answer was to squash everything that didn't align with the Law. This included loosey-goosey movements like the one associated with the wannabe Messiah named Jesus, so Paul put more than a little effort into stamping out this new community. He viewed it as a dangerous distraction that might further hinder God from finishing what he started.

But then Paul met Jesus. More specifically, Jesus knocked him off his horse and struck him with a light so bright he was blind for three days. And when Paul met Jesus, he began to discover that the entire story finds resolution here and here alone.

In yesterday's text, Paul didn't give us a reason to believe in Jesus so much as a reason not to not believe in Jesus. He answered the common objection that those who gave the world the gospel of Jesus shouldn't be trusted. But today he goes one further and begins building his case, starting with the realization that Jesus resolves the story of God as told in the first two-thirds of our Bibles.

We're looking again at the same passage from yesterday, and we're going to see that in it Paul highlights three ways Jesus fulfills the unfinished story of the Old Testament. The first is that in Christ the overall mystery is unveiled. Take a look at Colossians 1.25-27 and 2.2-3:

> *I became a servant according to the commission God gave me: to fill up the word of God for you,* **the mystery** *which was hidden from past ages and generations, but now has been made visible to those set apart. To them God chose to make known the richness of the glory of* **this mystery** *among the Gentiles,* **which is Christ in you**, *the hope of glory.*

> *I want them to come to all fullness of the full assurance of understanding and knowledge of* **the mystery of God, which is Christ**, *in whom are hidden all the treasures of wisdom and knowledge.*

Mystery doesn't refer to something currently unknown. It speaks about something previously unknown that has now come to light. It's like finding the lost key to a door no one could open. Here Paul makes the general point that as the Messiah, Jesus resolves the plot that the Old Testament leaves open. He is the key that unlocks the door of fulfillment for the story of God. We don't go to church wondering who the Messiah will be, or whether there will even be one. Why? Because the Messiah has already come.

Paul then gets a little more specific. His second point is that Jesus has solved the Gentile problem. "Gentile" simply means someone who is not a Jew. I'm guessing most of you fall into that category. Maybe you don't think it's strange that you worship the God of Israel. Maybe you take it for granted that when you put your faith in Jesus, you didn't have to take on the burden of following all 613 laws in the Old Testament. Well, it is strange, and we shouldn't take it for granted. You are a Gentile who worships the Jewish Messiah, but you didn't become a Jew to do so. Do you realize how ludicrous that was before Jesus? That fact alone should bolster your faith that something revolutionary happened in him. You don't just change centuries-old rules without being someone who matters!

Remember what Paul is doing: building a case that Jesus is who he says he is, that he stands at the pinnacle of God's mission to save us. Paul's final point from today's text lies in Colossians 2.3: *In him are hidden all the treasures of wisdom and knowledge.* Pause for a minute and think about that statement. Everything you need to know for life and godliness can be found right here. With this Paul answers the "How should we then live?" question. Where do *you* go for guidance? To whom do you turn when you need to know what to do? Before Jesus, God's people had one answer: the Law. They believed that all the treasures of God's wisdom were hidden in God's Law.[21] Paul disagrees, in part because he's experienced Law-following's dead end. And what Paul found true of the Law will prove true of anywhere you decide to turn except Jesus.

Consider yourself warned: Someone will come along and present you a non-Jesus option that sounds good. Don't be fooled. They'll claim to have a new key that unlocks a different treasure chest. Don't fall for it. Their promises will sound great, but when you get there you'll find a treasure box filled with moths and dust. You don't need any other source to tell you who God is, how his mission operates, or how to live.

Paul sums up the message he proclaims in one word: Christ. Why? Because only Christ resolves the true story of the true God. Our faith is centered not on an *it* but a *him*. What is Christianity? As Leonard Sweet and Frank Viola put it, "It is Christ. Nothing more. Nothing less. Christianity is not an ideology or a philosophy. Neither is it a new type of morality, social ethic, or worldview. Christianity is the 'good news' that beauty, truth, and goodness are found in a person. And true humanity and community are founded on and experienced by connection to that person."[22]

---

[21] You can see this, for instance, in 2 Baruch 44.14; 54.13.

[22] Sweet and Viola, xvi.

Paul offers this truth as both a comfort and a challenge. Be comforted in seeing that in Christ you have all that you need. Be challenged in knowing that you're barely scratching the surface of everything we find in him.

Competition
Chapter 17 – Colossians 2.4, 6-8

I currently have a toddler who (a) thinks I know everything and (b) believes she is always entitled to an explanation. So one of the most frequent words I hear these days is, "Why?" I've actually turned it into a game of sorts where I answer her question like I'm talking to another adult and then wait to see if she asks again. She typically does.

Trips to Target or the grocery store have become particularly entertaining, since she also thinks she needs anything colorful or cartoony. As a good father I deny her what she wants but doesn't need, and, of course, she asks why. In these situations my answers take on one of two forms. Either I explain that what she wants is not as great as she thinks: "No really, Claire, there's a reason that costs less than a dollar." Or I tell her that what she wants is not something that will add anything to the life she already enjoys: "You already have three monkeys and they're all cuter than that one."

For the next two days we're going to be exploring both of those concepts: overrating what we do not have and forgetting the superior value of what we already enjoy. It's as if Paul knows that his hearers then and now are going to look around and say, "Jesus is awesome but I want *that* too!" Paul, of course, answers with a "No," to which most of us will say, "Why?" Today we continue exploring Paul's answer.

Paul kind of throws down the gauntlet in this section and goes after whoever in Colossae was tempting the Colossian believers away from unalloyed allegiance to Jesus. At the beginning of 2.8, Paul warns his friends to *Be on guard so that no one takes you captive through some philosophy.* The word he uses for "take captive" refers to being kidnapped or carried off as an involuntary slave. Some scholars think that Paul has in mind a particular person doing the kidnapping; others suggest that a group of teachers is in mind. Either way, Paul now makes explicit what has remained under the surface up to this point: Someone is trying to pull the Colossian Christians away from the tradition they received about Jesus. So Paul calls them out. Publicly. Remember that most folks in the ancient world couldn't read, and the church would only have one copy of Paul's letter initially, so they would gather together and read it aloud. And at this point, everyone would know who Paul had in mind. It's like back in school when your teacher said, "One of you has been putting thumbtacks in my chair," while looking at the kid you all know did it. Uh-oh, someone's in trouble.

Paul isn't attacking philosophy in general. In his day the word "philosophy" simply meant any system of thought, sort of like we talk about our philosophy of dating or baseball. Paul considers this particular worldview to be a cheap substitute for genuine faith in Christ, and here he unfolds some of the reasons.

I tell you this so that none of you might be deceived by ideas that sound good on the surface. For I may be absent in flesh, but I am with you in Spirit, rejoicing and seeing your orderliness and the stability of your faith in Christ.

Therefore, just as you received Christ Jesus as Lord, continue walking in him, having been rooted and now being built up in him and being confirmed in the faith just as you were taught, overflowing with thanksgiving.

Be on guard so that no one takes you captive through some philosophy, some empty seduction that is based on human tradition, taking its cues from the elemental forces of the world rather than from Christ.

Paul is basically comparing Christ to the competition, and he finds the competition sorely lacking. Here he exposes five deficiencies in the teaching that competes with his own gospel, so let's look at each of them.

(1) This teaching only sounds good on the surface. It's not that these new ideas were completely stupid. It's not that wondering if we need more than Jesus is unheard of or a sign of complete buffoonery. Think about our day. Someone comes to you and says, "You don't need to look outside yourself to find salvation. The power that unlocks life's secret lies within you. Find peace not by looking out or up, but by looking in." At first glance this makes a little sense. We *are* powerful creatures and we *do* need to take personal responsibility for our own growth and development. But dig below the surface and this philosophy proves bankrupt, because thousands of years of human history – and a few hundred years of "secular humanism" – have taught us that we do not, in fact, possess the power to fix ourselves. Don't be deceived.

(2) This teaching is an empty seduction. Paul uses the Greek word *kenos*, which means empty, worthless, pointless; it is devoid of any real moral, intellectual, or spiritual value.[23] It seduces you with the promise of more but it doesn't actually add anything to your life.

(3) This teaching is based on human tradition. Here Paul takes his cues from Jesus, as well as the prophet Isaiah before him. God looked down at his people during Isaiah's day and concluded that instead of obeying his commands, they had decided to make up their own rules and act like they were obeying God. "The Lord says: 'These people come near to me with their mouth and honor me with their lips, but their hearts are far from me. Their worship of me is based on merely human rules they have been taught'" (Isaiah 29.13). Jesus quotes this verse to make the same point about God's people during his days on earth (see Mark 7.1-23). Someone once said, "God created us in his image, and then we returned the favor." Apparently this is a consistent temptation for us. Instead of receiving what God has actually revealed, we make up our own ideas and treat them like divine revelation.

(4) This teaching takes its cues from the elemental forces of the world. Welcome to one of the weirdest phrases in Colossians! Scholars have argued

---

[23] Douglas Moo, *The Letters to the Colossians and to Philemon* (Grand Rapids: Eerdmans, 2008), 186.

about this one for centuries, so we should hardly expect to solve the riddle here. The general gist is that Paul is saying this new teaching, which acts like it moves people forward, actually moves you backward. It's like if you were on a college baseball team and came to practice one day all excited to introduce your teammates to the concept of a double play. You'd get funny looks, to say the least. Why? Because everyone there has understood double plays since they were in kindergarten. Or to put it in musical terms, Paul says this is like moving from Handel's *Messiah* to saying your ABC's. It's the opposite of progress.

(5) *This teaching is not based on Christ.* For Paul this is the kicker, the tipping point, the final mark against the teaching he was attacking and against any other that claims to trump the truth about Jesus. You can't trump the Truth. Because God has revealed himself most clearly in Jesus, it just makes no sense to look elsewhere. The teaching you've heard about Jesus Christ as Lord is sufficient in every way.

Obviously this is built on everything Paul believes about Jesus. If we just take the book of Colossians, already we've found out that Jesus is the perfect revelation both of who God is and who we were created to be. His true gospel provides hope, redemption, and a future. He is the one in, through, and for whom everything was brought into existence, and he is more powerful than all of it. And he stands at the center of God's plan for restoring our broken world to beauty by reconciling all things to himself.

Some of you are still skeptical. "Okay fine, we get it that you and Paul believe some great things about Jesus. But Buddhists believe great things about the Buddha, Muslims believe great things about Muhammad, and New Agers love their mystics and seers. Everyone has their heroes, their holy ones, their prophets and teachers, or at least their sacred ideas. What makes Jesus so special?"

I want to add two more subpoints to Paul's case for the uniqueness of Jesus. First, nowhere else will you find the same combination of *claims* and *character*. Jesus claimed to stand at the very center of God's purposes for creation; he even subtly claimed to be the human incarnation of God himself. Jesus also was by all counts a man of high character. His enemies had to make up stuff about him in order to get him crucified, and even then there were no questions raised about his morality or integrity. No one said, "Jesus talks about peace but he's actually a murderer." Or, "Jesus talks about sexual purity but what about all those mistresses?"

You will find other leaders who claim to stand at the center of God's revelation. You'll find men who claim to be God's true prophet, or even God in the flesh. And you will find people of high character, such as Mother Teresa or Gandhi or your faithful grandmother. But you will not find both. Unless you're looking at Jesus.[24]

And the second point I want to remind you of is that Jesus was raised from the dead. I once heard about a young man who grew up in a Buddhist context but had recently heard the message of Jesus. He was torn. He spent days in prayer and study but couldn't make a decision. Then one night he had a dream. In this dream he was walking down a path and came to a fork in the road. To the left he saw Buddha, who was, well, dead. To the right he saw Jesus, who was, well, alive. You can probably guess what decision he made when he woke up.

If you are tempted to walk away from Jesus and toward some other teaching or habit or way of life, you need to remember that the philosophy you're considering is overrated. And you must not forget that the one you're walking away from has no equal.

---

[24] Vinoth Ramachandra, *Faiths in Conflict* (Downers Grove: IVP Academic, 2000), 87-118. You should seriously read Ramachandra's chapter on Jesus. The entire book is great, but that chapter is one of the best single chapter treatments of Jesus I've come across.

Fullness
Chapter 18 – Colossians 2.9

I expected everything to change when I became a dad. I assumed it would impact how I watched movies and listened to music, where I wanted to live and why, how I viewed things like the American school system, the future of our economy, and what clothes our culture tells girls to wear in order to be pretty.

My expectations were not disappointed. Everything looks different now, Jesus included. I thought holding Claire and learning to love her through the process of becoming a full-grown human person would give me a new appreciation for the depth of God's patience and joy and love. It has. But it has also changed the way I hear the challenges of Jesus.

I used to think Jesus' extreme demands were impressive.

If you want to be my disciple, you must deny yourself, take up your cross daily and follow me. For whoever wants to save their life will lose it, but whoever loses their life for me and for the gospel will save it.

If anyone comes to me and does not hate father and mother, wife and children, brothers and sisters—yes, even their own life—such a person cannot be my disciple.

Anyone who loves their father or mother more than me is not worthy of me; anyone who loves their son or daughter more than me is not worthy of me.

Now I find them terrifying.

Up to the point of fatherhood, loving Jesus so much that I hated others by comparison seemed noble and exciting. Holding a little girl who will spend the rest of her life calling me "daddy" makes that kind of sacrifice seem irresponsible and wrong. How is it okay to give someone a gift as precious as a child and then demand that the child be marginalized?

Whether you're more like the old me or the new me, you have to admit that Jesus can be uncomfortably bold. He doesn't want some of you. He wants all of you. Jesus calls for unqualified allegiance. Jesus demands unlimited devotion.

Audacity seems to be one characteristic Jesus passed on to Paul. Paul doesn't fit well in our world where tolerance is the prized virtue. It's not that Paul is mean. He just doesn't pull any punches. He thinks Jesus is better than any potential competitor. Today we continue understanding why.

What Paul says about Jesus in today's text might be the most elevated words written about Jesus in the entire Bible: *For in him dwells all the fullness of Deity in bodily form.* It doesn't get any more exalted than that. Paul claims in no uncertain terms that Jesus is God in human form. He actually builds on something he said back in 1.19: *In him all the Fullness was pleased to permanently dwell.* We talked about this a bit in the *Visibility* chapter, but what Paul left vague back then he states here as clearly as possible. It's not merely that Jesus makes God visible. That's 100% true, but there's more. In Jesus we not only see what God is like, we actually make contact with God himself. Or better yet, God establishes personal contact with us. In *Braveheart*, Mel Gibson showed us what William Wallace was like. But you could watch the movie a dozen times and you still wouldn't know William Wallace as well as if you actually spent time with him. Jesus is God spending time with us. Jesus is God playing himself in a movie.

Let's break down Paul's statement beginning with a word not found in 1.19: "Deity." We need to get technical for just a minute because sometimes details matter. The root word Paul uses for Deity is *theotēs*, which has a fraternal twin in the word *theiotēs*. The only difference is literally one iota, but this iota separates being like God from actually being God. *Theiotēs* means that you have the characteristics or qualities of God. This is great, but it doesn't mean you're actually Deity. *Theotēs*, on the other hand, means "the state of being God." Jesus isn't just *like* God; Jesus actually is God.

As if the word isn't enough, Paul adds that the *fullness* of Deity dwells in Jesus. You get the sense Paul doesn't want to be misunderstood here! You don't find a little bit of God in Jesus and a little bit of God in your ancestors and another little bit of God in yourself. It all dwells in one place. And do note that Paul says it *dwells* in Jesus. Not dwelt for a while and then hiked off to some other place. Deity took up residence in Jesus *permanently*.

The Bible is very clear that God can dwell wherever he wants. In the past God had chosen to dwell on a particular mountain – Mount Sinai (also known as Mount Zion). Israel's songwriters celebrated this fact time and again in the book of Psalms. "For the LORD has chosen Zion, he has desired it for his dwelling" (Psalm 132.13). In Psalm 68.18, the writer basically tells other mountains not to be jealous: "Mount Bashan, majestic mountain, Mount Bashan, rugged mountain, why gaze in envy, you rugged mountain, at the mountain where God chooses to reign, where the LORD himself will dwell forever?" Ancient faith also teaches that God chose to dwell in a tent that moved with the people, in the Temple of Jerusalem, or in the words of Israel's prophets.

God freely chose to dwell in these places, and when Israel didn't keep her side of the bargain, God freely chose to withdraw his presence. But in Jesus, God takes things to a new level because he chooses to permanently dwell in a person. God has not chosen to permanently dwell in a building. God has not chosen to permanently dwell in a book. God has chosen to dwell *in a body* – the body of one man: Jesus of Nazareth, who has become our Savior, Lord, and King. He is not just one leader among many. He is not just a moralist or social revolutionary. He is not just another self-help guru. He is not just one more way up the mountain; he is the top of the mountain personally travelling down to the valley below. You don't need to look anywhere else to access divine reality or experience spiritual fullness.

You want more? Excellent. You don't need to hedge your bets or spread your allegiance just to make sure you align with the winner. The winner is already in your midst. The logic is very simple: if you want the ocean, go to the coast. If you want money, go to the ATM. If you want skyscrapers, go to New York City or Tokyo. If you want God, go to the one in whom the fullness of Deity chose to permanently dwell. I'd say this qualifies as a no-brainer. Who could be more capable or better equipped?

Forgive me for hitting the same drum again, but all you need is more of what you already have been given. All you need is more Jesus.

Biography
Chapter 19 – Colossians 2.10-12

Why do we read other people's stories? Why do we watch movies that tell true accounts of people's lives? We watch them because we love stories – inspiring stories, depressing stories, bizarre stories. We read them because truth really is stranger than fiction. We pay attention because people fascinate us. We want to know how people get from where they begin to where they finish.

We read and watch biographies to satisfy a need deeper than mere curiosity. Typically without even knowing it, we seek connections between their stories and ours. Characters we relate to, wish we could be, or fear we might become. Plot lines not too dissimilar from our own – loves both won and lost, responsibilities both celebrated and resented, adventures both aborted and as-yet-incomplete. Aches and joys and fears and dreams from our past, our present, or (we wonder) our future.

All the best stories come alive in precisely this fashion. All the best stories find a place for us in the telling. In today's text Paul tells our story within Jesus' story.

You are in him where you have already been made complete. He is the head of all rule and authority. And in him you were circumcised with a circumcision not done by human hands, but by stripping off the body of flesh in the circumcision of Christ, having been buried with him in baptism. In him you were also raised, through the faithful working of God who raised him from the dead. And though you were dead in your transgressions and in the uncircumcision of your flesh, he made you alive together with him.

Paul aims to bolster our confidence not in ourselves but in what God has done for us in Jesus. And what God has done for us in Jesus is to incorporate us into what he has done in Jesus. Paul lays out the contours of Jesus' life in simplest form: he lived, he underwent a death and burial, and God then raised him from the dead to a new type of life altogether. This is the story of Jesus, and as far as God is concerned the story of Jesus is your story too. If you asked God to write your biography, this would be the plotline. God has written us into the narrative of Jesus' death and resurrection.

Confused? Don't worry, you're not alone! Even the great Apostle Peter had a hard time following Paul's logic at times (2 Peter 3.15-16). Keep reading and we'll see if we can make some sense of what all this means.

Imagine that you are a word and Jesus is book full of blank pages. Essentially God has written us into the book's blank pages, so that whatever happens to the book happens to the words. If the book is placed on a library shelf, the words sit on the shelf too. If the book is checked out from the library, the words leave too. If the book is shipped from a library in Joplin to one in Jerusalem, the words add a little international travel to their resume.

Imagine that you are a bundle of cash and Jesus is a safe. God has basically locked a bunch of cash bundles in a safe, so that whatever happens to the safe happens to the cash. Imagine you are a child and your father or mother gets a new job in Portland. Guess what? You're moving to Portland. Perhaps more to the point of what Paul had in mind, imagine you are a citizen in a country and your army goes out to battle a hostile enemy. If your army emerges victorious, you too taste the benefits of victory. What happened to Jesus has echoed in us.

With all this in mind – knowing that in these verses Paul is telling our story within Jesus' story – let's investigate what he actually says. For starters, notice that he's talking about our baptism. Biblically speaking, baptism is primarily about us publicly joining God's family by being united to Jesus in death and resurrection. Think about the act of baptism itself. We are dipped down into water, where it is dark and cold and quiet – kind of like death. Then we are raised back up out of the water-grave to a brand new life. We could explore this basic imagery in any number of ways – for instance, we could talk about how the water dripping off of us symbolizes the cleansing that God has effected in our souls, or how the fact that we're baptized by someone else represents the idea that baptism is less about what we do and more about what God does in us. But here Paul focuses on the movement from death to life, both of which have positive connotations in this case.

First he talks about death, and to illustrate what happens in this death he relies on the ancient practice of circumcision. Here again is the sentence: *In him you were circumcised with a circumcision not done by human hands, but by stripping off the body of flesh in the circumcision of Christ.* Circumcision of course refers to the cutting off of a particular piece of skin, but here Paul speaks metaphorically of *stripping off the body of flesh.* Scholars debate what Paul means here, but there is little confusion once we realize that Paul is speaking of two things at the same time. Somewhat strangely, he refers to Christ's death as a circumcision in which Christ's fleshly body was literally put to death. But the second meaning is related to Paul's typical use of the word "flesh" – the part of our humanity that is mortal, weak, susceptible to sin's seduction. In other places he talks about how we fight against the flesh, which means we fight against our desires to revert to a worldly way of life rather than the ways of Jesus. Though they are a gift from God and essentially good, in this fallen world our bodies often work against us because we are not yet wise and strong enough to tame their desires.

However, Paul says here that a transformation occurred when we became followers of Jesus. It's as if in some mysterious way God reached down into the core of our being and flipped a switch, so that our deepest motivations are no longer against God but for God. It's not that we are no longer tempted, but the power in us working for good is now stronger and more fundamental than the power working for evil.

I'm actually getting ahead of Paul a bit. So far all he has said is that the "do evil" switch has been turned off. We experience the bit of fleshly electricity still coursing through the lines, but the supply has been cut off and the power is dwindling. We no longer want the same ungodly things as much as we did before. We're no longer powerless to resist those desires. We no longer have to be imprisoned by the same worries or fears as before.

But that's just the first half. Paul goes on to say that in addition to pulling the evil plug, God has injected into our spiritual bloodstream something powerfully positive: life. *In him you were also raised, through the faithful working of God who raised him from the dead. And though you were dead in your transgressions and in the uncircumcision of your flesh, he made you alive together with him.* Our engines have switched from one kind of fuel to another.[25] Our spiritual DNA has been forever altered because a new source of life flows through the deepest parts of our being.

Let's reflect for a minute on the nature of "life." Life is basically the ability to draw resources from the surrounding world in order to grow up. We say seeds are alive because they send out roots into the surrounding soil in order to draw in nutrients that will enable them to become flowers. For humans to be alive means that we feed off our environment. Passively, we breathe. We don't try to breathe or tell ourselves to breathe; we just naturally draw in oxygen and allow it to keep our body going. Actively, we eat and drink. If we stop eating or drinking or (especially) breathing, we will die.

By aligning our story with the story not only of Jesus' death but also his resurrection, God has provided us a new environment full of ingredients for a new kind of life, as well as the new spiritual ability to draw in resources from that environment. I know it sounds crazy, but how else do you explain the transformation we've seen in people who give their lives to Christ? How else do we explain the changes we've noticed in ourselves? We're far from perfect, but the more we pursue Jesus, the more we find that we actually want the things that God has told us to desire.

Why does Paul say all this? Because he wants us to know, as he said at the beginning of today's passage, that we are *in Christ where we have already been made complete.* Nothing is needed that we haven't already been given. We have been liberated from bondage to evil and plugged in to the power of a life that is truly good. Jesus' biography has become our autobiography. We will never find a better story than the one to which we've already been joined in him.

---

[25] Dallas Willard, *The Spirit of the Disciplines* (New York: Harper Collins, 1990), 114.

Release

Chapter 20 – Colossians 2.13-14

I know a guy who always finds a way to talk about his wife's menopause. Doesn't matter the topic or context or time of day. It always comes back to menopause. It was awkward at first, but in my ornerier moments it became a sort of game. I'd start a conversation with him about shoes, electricity, or the Lakers, and try to predict how long before he'd recall his experience of walking with his wife through these trying years. It's amazing how many metaphors he pulled from this singularly life-changing experience.

Not to be too crass, but what menopause is for my friend, Christ's crucifixion is for Paul. He can't stop talking about it. Start a conversation with Paul about drum kits or a glass of milk or politics or women, and eventually he'll turn it into an exposition of the cross. It's not quite as awkward as menopause but it is every bit as noticeable, and in this regard today's portion of Colossians doesn't disappoint.

Remember, Paul is telling us that we don't require more of anything except Jesus. He is sufficient. He is enough. In him we are complete. He has accomplished everything anyone needs to accomplish to secure our life and wellbeing and to guide us along paths of righteousness and peace. Jesus plus nothing equals everything.[26] Today and tomorrow we're going to

---

[26] This particular phrase comes from Tullian Tchividjian's *Jesus + Nothing = Everything* (Wheaton: Crossway, 2011).

unpack the way he brings the present bit of his argument to a close. Here's the first half in Colossians 2.13b-14:

Having graciously forgiven us all our transgressions, having erased the debt record which was against us with its decrees that opposed us; he has done away with it, having nailed it to the cross.

I hope you've never uttered the words, "I have no regrets." People who say they have no regrets in life are either lying, have no conscience, or don't understand the consequences of human behavior. I don't mean to be harsh and I'm sorry if I've hurt your feelings. It's just that when used about life as a whole, this seemingly innocent phrase reveals one of our most dangerous blind spots: We don't take seriously the amount of evil we've added to the world.

I think the problem is that we haven't thought it through. We're not unaware that our actions have hurt people – some in ways we can see, others not so much – but for some reason we don't connect the dots from that knowledge to appropriate feelings of regret.

It's not hard to figure out why. The reason is probably that we can't bear facing the truth. It's painful to acknowledge the ways our mistakes have hurt others. Real life doesn't offer do-overs or mulligans. So often our misdoings become demons that we eventually deal with by denying their negative impact, but there's just no way to avoid the solemn truth that actions have consequences.

Imagine your family is experiencing hard times financially. Simply put, you need money or drastic changes will have to be made. After stressing for weeks and then months with no leads to pursue, you become aware of a possible promotion at work. Your odds improve when you find out you're on the short list for the new gig, which will provide enough extra income to avoid uprooting the kids and moving in with your dysfunctional in-laws. The only problem is that one of your colleagues is the other finalist, and you know he's a better fit for the new position. Your boss pulls you into his office and asks you straight up what you think of this other person. You've been working together for years, so few know him better. At that point you're facing a dilemma as old as humanity: tell the truth and likely forego what you want, or lie and meet the immediate need.

Whatever you do in this moment will create ripples. Whatever action you take will set in motion a chain of consequences that you probably won't be able to control – consequences not only for you but for your family as a whole, for the company, for this other man, his family and career, and so on.

Each of us, metaphorically speaking, has told the lie. Not just once, but at multiple points in our lives. Each of us has contributed to the mess that is our world in its present form.

What do you do with that? How do you sleep at night with the realization that you're part of the problem? Maybe you're not as bad as child predators or murderers or even adulterers, but you too have caused others pain that could have been avoided, not to mention the fact that you've grieved the very heart of God.

You may wonder what all this has to do with Colossians and specifically with today's verses. Actually these realities were very much part of the problem in Colossae. Some of the Colossian Christians did take seriously the painful effect of their mistakes, so much so that they couldn't stop looking for ways to get rid of their guilt. This is part of why they turned to other religious rituals and experiences, but Paul says that this, too, is an unnecessary move when you understand what Christ has done for us.

Let's focus on the phrase *the debt record which was against us with its decrees that opposed us*. What does this mean? Scholars debate the precise details, but most agree on the basic idea: This is an I.O.U.-type document that we signed but then failed to pay, and now the courts are calling and demanding reimbursement. It could be that Paul has in mind the Law that God gave Israel. Or he could be thinking more generally of the moral code that has been imprinted in all of our souls. Either way, the point is that we all have known what to do but haven't done it. We've sinned. We've failed. And now we must account for the debt.

What will we do with our unpaid and unpayable I.O.U.? That's the question Paul raises, and it's one we do well to personally consider. Thankfully Paul immediately answers by explaining what Jesus did with it. Paul says that Jesus *erased* it. The word comes from wiping away the letters from a wax tablet. You can no longer read our sin-list because it's *gone*. The witness against us has been dismissed from the courtroom. What's more, Jesus has *done away with it*. It's like he erased your sins out of a book, and then burned the book for good measure. Paul then specifies how – or maybe we should say *where* – Jesus accomplished this. Thanks specifically to Jesus' death on the cross, no case can be raised against us.

So let's revisit our question: What will we do with our unpaid and unpayable debt? So far as I can tell we have five options:

(1) We can *deny* it and live a lie. It is possible to pretend that we haven't done anything *that* wrong, that there really is no problem to solve. For a while. I'd guess many of you are walking this path, and while I feel for you, I do hope you see soon that if you've reached the point where this lie feels true, you are in a very dangerous place.

(2) We can *embrace* it and go wild. It is what it is, we might say, and there's nothing we can do about it now. And if we've already missed the boat, we might as well throw a party on this side of the water. The self-hatred embodied in this option is only a few feet below the surface. Please don't waste your time and damage your heart by learning this the hard way.

(3) We could *bear* it and learn to live with guilt. Unfortunately this is probably the most common path, and it always leads to more heartache. Typically our loved ones feel the brunt, as we often try to ensure that everyone around is perfect so we feel better about the fact that we're not.

(4) We could *doubt* Jesus and seek another solution. This is the option some in Colossae had chosen, and it's basically another version of number three. Sometimes people walk away from Jesus altogether and revert to one of the first two options. But more often we supplement Jesus' offer of forgiveness with some form of "works righteousness" – we try to do enough good deeds to outweigh the bad. It's a painful and blinding cycle that I do not recommend.

(5) We could *release* the burden of our debt and live in peace.

This last option requires that we take Jesus at his word and accept his sacrifice on our behalf, which for some reason isn't always easy. But it is nonetheless the option based in truth. In the divine courtroom, no one has any basis for accusations against you. Why? Because Jesus paid it all.

Trust in the sufficiency of Christ's death on the cross. Be freed from the burden of guilt over what you know full well you've done wrong. Walk in the joy of this forgiveness that begins now and stretches into life eternal.

Exposure
Chapter 21 – Colossians 2.15

Danish storyteller Hans Christian Anderson once wrote about an ancient emperor who cared about nothing but his clothes. He demanded the finest clothes in the land, and he cut no corners in showing them off. Sometimes, after receiving a new outfit, he would parade through his land just so everyone could see and praise his breathtaking apparel.

One day, two men approached the emperor with the news that they could use special new cloth to make the finest suit of clothes that anyone had ever seen. These clothes were so remarkable, the two men added, that they were only visible to people of high quality and intelligence. The clothes could not be seen by anyone who was stupid or beneath the emperor's dignity.

The king was naturally nervous about whether *he* would be able to see the clothes, so he sent his two top advisors to take a look. Neither wanted to admit they weren't smart enough to see, so they lied and said the suit was indeed indescribably beautiful. By this time other folks throughout the land heard about the clothes, and all were eager to see which of their neighbors were too stupid to see.

Though tragically the emperor himself could not see them, he wasn't about to admit his insufficiency. So he allowed himself to be dressed with the new clothes for a parade. Everyone lined the streets and shouted aloud how stunning his new clothes were, each of them afraid to admit the truth.

But then a child peeked her head through the front of the crowd and yelled aloud for all to hear, "The emperor has no clothes!"[27]

Powerful people have a way of convincing others that they should never be questioned. Children have a knack for cutting through pretense and laying bare the truth. In today's verse, Paul takes the childlike approach and exposes every powerful being in heaven and earth.

Having disarmed the rulers and authorities, he publicly exposed them, having led them in a Triumphal Procession in him.

– Colossians 2.15

This isn't the first time we've met *rulers and authorities* in this letter, so let's review the three points we know so far.

(1) We are dealing with both heavenly and earthly rulers and authorities (1.16). To put it simply, Paul's phrase encompasses what we cannot see (i.e. Satan, demons, false gods) as well as what we can see (i.e. emperors, governors, priests). Essentially every person or position of power is included in this phrase.

(2) All *rulers and authorities* – both the people in power and the powerful positions they're in – have been created in Christ, through Christ, and to serve Christ. He is their rightful ruler, the King of Kings so to speak (1.16).

(3) The rulers and authorities rebelled, though, so Jesus had to reconcile them to himself – bring them back into submission to their rightful king

---

[27] Hans Christian Andersen, *Fairy Tales of Hans Christian Andersen* (Oxford: Oxford University Press, 1959), 107-113.

– through his death and resurrection (1.20). Jesus did this and is therefore *the head of all rule and authority* (2.10).

Paul doesn't hesitate to assert Jesus' victory over all rulers and authorities, but up to this point he hasn't really explained how this came to be. Now he (finally!) does.

By his death and resurrection, Jesus *disarmed* and *exposed* the rulers and authorities. To "disarm" means just what you'd think – to remove or neutralize someone else's weapons. The verb "expose" means making someone's true colors known to the watching world. It was used, for instance, in an ancient custom of cutting off an adulteress's hair and treating her like a prostitute. It's also the word used in Matthew 1.19 to describe Joseph not wanting to subject the Virgin Mary to public disgrace by telling everyone that she became pregnant by someone else while engaged to him.

Paul adds a third image to disarm and expose: Jesus led his defeated enemies in a *Triumphal Procession*. "Triumphs," as the Romans called them, were public parades where victorious emperors and generals would caravan through Rome with their defeated captors in tow. It was basically a public mockery of the losers and celebration of the victors. It wasn't so much the victory itself as much as a party commemorating the victory.

How was the cross, which by all normal evaluations looked like pathetic defeat, actually both a victory and the celebration of a victory? How did Jesus *disarm* and *expose* both heavenly and earthly rulers and authorities? By neutralizing their greatest weapons: the power to accuse, the pretense of innocence, and the power to threaten us with death.[28] Let's look at each of these in turn.

First, by sacrificing himself for our sins, Jesus removed any basis for accusation against you and me. The name "Satan" actually means *Accuser*, but because of Jesus, our Accuser has nothing to say against us in the courts of God. Jesus took upon himself the wrath of God that you and I deserve so that we don't have to experience it. Our debt has been settled once and for all. So our enemy can no longer use our guilt against us by constantly reminding us of what we've done wrong. He can and does try to use our sins to make us feel worthless and thus give up on following Jesus, but his

---

[28] I'm sure there are more, but these are the ones we're going to explore today.

accusations ring hollow to the extent that we understand what Jesus has accomplished.

Second, one of the ways powerful beings – demonic, political, and religious – maintain control is by people giving them the benefit of the doubt. Why do you think so many normal German Christians compromised their obedience to Jesus by supporting – or at least turning a blind eye toward – such heinous massacring of the Jews? Why do you suppose so many worshipers of God throughout history – Christians included, unfortunately – believed leaders who claimed that God wanted them to kill folks for disagreeing? And why in the world would otherwise sane and normal human beings flirt with something as uncontrollable as spiritual evil? Because in all these cases, people were deceived into believing that there was no way these rulers and authorities were not safe and good.

It's easy for us to point to examples like this, though, because we're talking about *those* people. We're talking about corruption that is so obvious we'd never fall into the same trap.

Not so fast. Jesus went up against the best of the best. As one author put it, "Jesus was executed not by some frenzied mob or rogue justice, but by the best religion, the most powerful state, and the most perfect legal system, functioning as they were each designed to do." [29] This religion full of extreme devotion to God, combined with a government as sleek and streamlined as any history has seen, actually met God in the flesh. And what did they do to him? They put him to death. No longer could they pretend to have humanity's best interests in mind. No longer could they claim to represent the priorities and policies of God. Jesus exposed their deceit and wakes us up to the fact that the people in charge might not always be on the side of good.

Third, Jesus disarms the rulers and authorities by displaying the weakness of their last and greatest weapon: death. Hebrews articulates this point in a little more detail: *Since the children have flesh and blood, Jesus too shared in their humanity so that he might break the power of him who holds the power of death – that is, the devil – and free those who all their lives were held in slavery by their fear of death* (2.14-15). Let's make sense of this by working from human rulers to spiritual ones. How do human authorities get people to do their will? By threatening them, the worst threat being that if you cross

---

[29] Sweet and Viola, 112.

the wrong line, you will die. Our fear of death keeps us in line. The same is true of demonic powers: they convince us that if we don't listen, we'll either literally lose our lives or at least they'll no longer be worth living. Power feeds on fear. Yet Jesus wasn't afraid to die, even though he had the power to stop those putting him to death. Why? Because he knew that God cannot be stopped by something as weak as death. He knew that God raises the dead, overcoming death and removing the ominous power of its threat to humanity.

What difference does all this make? Two final thoughts. First, never listen to anyone who tells you that Jesus isn't enough to secure you God's forgiveness. This is of course the point Paul made in yesterday's passage, but it bleeds over into today as well. Jesus has exposed each and every accuser, whether human or demonic, by doing everything necessary to reconcile us to God.

Second, no one except Jesus has the absolute and unquestionable right to tell you what to do. No ruler has authority that is independent of the one who is the head of all rule and authority. I don't mean that we don't have to submit to legitimate authority. On the contrary, the Bible is very clear that we do. We are called to submit to the authority of our parents and our teachers and our governments – so long as what they tell us to do doesn't violate what *Jesus* has told us to do. If and when it does, Jesus wins. Every time.

And with that, Paul closes his case for our confidence that in Jesus we enjoy absolutely everything we need for life, fulfillment, and growth.

moreJESUS part 4 – GROWTH

One time, while enjoying a dinner party, Albert Einstein was approached by a college student who didn't recognize him. She asked what the old scientist did by profession. "I am a student of physics," Einstein answered. "Still? Even at your age?" the student replied, and then added, "I finished physics two years ago."

Never assume that you are done growing. Don't think that God doesn't want you to develop, mature, spiritually evolve. This could not be further from the truth. Don't think that your thirst for more means you are immature or selfish or lacking contentment. Your thirst for more means you are spiritually alive. Let me say this as clearly as possible: God wants us to grow into more than we currently are.

Up to this point, Paul has gone out of his way to reassure us that we already have everything we need in Jesus. Don't be confused though. He isn't saying no more growth is needed. He's simply mapping out for us the only route that will lead us to the proper destination.

Notice the following verses from Colossians that speak of hope for growth and encouragement to reach fullness and maturity:

This [faith, love, and hope] you previously heard about in the true message of the gospel, which has come to you just as in all the world it is bearing fruit and growing. It has done the same thing in you from the first day you heard and came to know the truth of God's grace.

Because of this, from the first day we heard about you we have not stopped praying for you and asking that you be filled with the knowledge of God's will in all Spiritual wisdom and understanding, so that you may walk in a manner worthy of the Lord that pleases him in every way: bearing fruit in every kind of good work and growing in the knowledge of God.

I became a servant [of the church] according to the commission God gave me: to fill up the word of God for you.

[Christ] is the one we publicly proclaim, admonishing everyone and teaching everyone in all wisdom, so that we might present everyone mature in Christ.

I want them to come to all fullness of the full assurance of understanding and knowledge of the mystery of God, which is Christ, in whom are hidden all the treasures of wisdom and knowledge.

Therefore, just as you received Christ Jesus as Lord, continue walking in him, having been rooted and now being built up in him.

The head, from whom the whole body – nourished and woven together by its joints and muscles – grows with the growth that comes from God.

But also notice the assumption behind this last one: There are many kinds of so-called "growth," and most of them don't come from God.

Most parents give their children more vegetables than candy. Why? Because we know by both instinct and experience that there is a right way and a wrong way to help your kids reach physical health and maturity.

Most successful students study over long periods of time rather than cram a semester-full of information at the last minute. Why? Because we know that there is a right way and a wrong way not only to ace a test but also to actually retain information in our long-term memory.

Most talented musicians practice their craft more than a few times per week. Why? Because we know that without following certain principled habits we will never reach high levels of proficiency.

Same goes for sports and painting and driving a car. There are right ways to learn these skills, and there are countless ways to learn them wrong. And the same is true for a life of discipleship. Growth in true spirituality is not attained just any old way. There is a path that comes from God, and many impostors try to draw us off it.

Throughout this next section of Colossians, Paul teaches us how to stay the course. At this point in the letter, the "more Jesus" theme becomes more background than foreground. Paul has essentially made his case that all we need is more of what we already have – all we need is more Jesus – so now he will unpack for us what pursuing this kind of more actually looks like.

Here is how the second half of Colossians will unfold. This week we'll talk specifically about the kind of growth God is working in us. After exploring some typical temptations of living spiritually, we'll get the proper framework in our minds. Then we'll talk about the power behind actual transformation and discuss the seriousness, motivation, goal, and process of ridding ourselves of the old life and overflowing with the new. God's growth plan directly spills over into next week, where we'll discuss the actual context for growing up in Jesus: our relationships with others in the church. Then we'll wrap up by learning how a life of more is a life of mission, exploring Paul's closing thoughts on engaging outsiders so they, too, come to see all that is available in Jesus.

Hazards
Chapter 22 – Colossians 2.16-23

One of my college professors often warned us about "occupational hazards." The idea is basically that whatever profession you enter brings with it certain inbuilt dangers or temptations. If you become a professional baseball pitcher, for instance, then you are more likely to experience injuries to your throwing shoulder or elbow. If you go into counseling, there is a chance that you'll become emotionally detached from people's problems or pessimistic about whether folks will take the steps necessary to achieve psychological health. A successful career in modeling might create in you the expectation that your good looks can get you whatever you want in life; or on the other hand, the same profession might produce paralyzing insecurity since so much depends on meeting impossible standards of perfection.

The concept actually stretches beyond occupations and professions. Any pursuit in life positions you for certain kinds of positive growth as well as certain negative tendencies. Becoming a history buff might make you think you're smarter than other people and thus breed arrogance. Losing large amounts of weight, while generally a positive transformation, sometimes causes tension in relationships as two people learn to adjust to such dramatic change.

Religion has its own occupational hazards, and not just for professional pastors or priests. All who attempt to deal with the divine must beware.

This is true even for those who don't "believe." Generally speaking, when it comes to religion folks fall into one of three categories, each with their own specific temptations. Atheists have a tendency to perceive themselves as more rational and less given to emotional theological commitments than others, even in cases where the opposite is true. Agnostics – those unsure whether or not God exists – easily fall into the trap of assuming the God question doesn't really matter. Actually nothing is further from the truth because if God does exist, then we'd be exceedingly dumb not to pay him mind.

Then there's the third group: believers. To understand our occupational hazard, consider where "religion" comes from. In many ways, ancient religion – in the sense of intentional and organized worship of God or gods – began on the farm. Imagine yourself in need of crops and at the mercy of forces you can neither explain nor control – weather, soil cycles, etc. What else could you do but cry out to the skies in an attempt to tap in to whatever power will provide what you need? Various gods and goddesses were invented to govern life-giving or life-destroying resources: the sun, the sea, the seasons, hunting success, etc. All of these forces or "gods and goddesses" needed to be either pleased or placated so as to ensure a long and prosperous life.

By Paul's day the traditional gods began giving way to astrology, oracles, or magic, all of which employ the same logic: Find the right formula to unlock divine power so you get what you need. Discover the correct words to utter or rituals to undergo, and the gods will work in your favor.

Or so we tend to think. More than anything else, this is the "occupational hazard" of worshiping God – the desire to do whatever is necessary to get God on our side. On more than one occasion I have refused to baptize people even though they asked for it. Why? Because they don't really want to hand over their lives to Jesus as Lord. They just wanted him to fix something: marriage, kids, health, career. We've all been in situations where we want something *so bad* that finally we make the ultimate promise, "God, I will do anything. Just please, please, please (fill in the blank). Name your price and I'll pay it."

Typically we avoid that degree of bluntness. Sometimes we don't even know we're playing this game. We just quietly perform whatever duties we think God wants and hope for the best.

Our search for the right formula often falls into one of a few standard patterns. Let's look at the four Paul criticizes in Colossians 2.16-23:

Therefore, don't let anyone pass judgment on you regarding food and drink, or because of feasts, new moon celebrations, or sabbaths. All these are a shadow of the things that were to come – the reality is Christ. Let no one rule against you who delights in humility and angelic worship, which he has seen upon entering a visionary trance. He is vainly inflated by the mind of his flesh and isn't holding fast to the head, from whom the whole body – nourished and woven together by its joints and muscles – grows with the growth that is from God.

If you died with Christ from the elemental forces of the world, why, as though living in the world, do you submit to its regulations? "Do not handle! Do not taste! Do not touch!" All these are destined to perish in their use, and are based on human commands and teachings. Though they have an appearance of wisdom in their self-imposed worship, humility, and harsh treatment of the body, they are completely worthless and serve only to indulge the flesh.

First we need to remember that Paul was dealing with a specific problem in Colossae. As we have learned, some in Colossae felt the need to supplement Jesus with other spiritual pursuits. Wise to cover all the bases, they figured. Best we can tell from today's passage and others, they were pursuing visionary experiences during which they were caught up to "heavenly realms" where they either worshiped angels or worshiped God along with the angels. They considered such visions marks of their spiritual maturity and taught that, in order to qualify, you needed to maintain a strict religious calendar built around festivals, the practice of fasting, and avoiding certain creaturely benefits (like certain foods, for instance).

Paul does not approve.

This probably isn't the precise recipe you and I find tempting, so we're going to examine Paul's critique and identify four religious hazards that enticed God's people then and today. Paul first goes after the most basic formula: ritual. He mentions *food and drink, feasts, new moon celebrations,* and *sabbaths.* As rituals so often become, these practices were part of an attempt to nail down the correct procedure or formula for accessing God's favor.

Rituals were highly valued and structured in Paul's day. Check out this warning from Roman lawyer Pliny the Younger: "The text for invoking a happy omen is different from that for averting an ill or that for making a request. The highest officials pray in fixed forms of words, and to make sure that not a word is omitted or spoken in the wrong place, a prompter read the text before them, another person is appointed to watch over it, yet another to command silence, and the flute-player plays to mask all other sounds."[30]

We could replace these items with attending church the right amount of times per week, reading our Bibles regularly, or throwing the right religious parties at the correct times of the year. These things are fine and good in their own right, but not when they become part of the "list" or formula we use to manipulate God into blessing us.

The second temptation is to evaluate our faithfulness to God based on spiritual experiences. "I prayed for an hour and just *felt* God's presence in the room with me." "God often speaks to me through dreams." "The Lord speaks to me every day." Again, all these things are good and legitimate ways God communicates to his people, but the temptation is to open our eyes, look in the mirror, and say, "Hey, God just warmed your heart or showed you some great stuff. You must be pretty awesome." As we will see throughout this and next week, God is more interested in how we treat others than in what we experience when we're all alone.

The third temptation, which is really more of a distraction, enjoys as much popularity today as ever: angels. To this day the most popular message I've given at our current church was one on angels. On the one hand, this probably owes to the fact that our culture pushes a bunch of ideas about angels that are flat out unbiblical, and people are glad to hear some actual truth on the matter. But on the other hand, for whatever reason angels seem more accessible to us than Jesus, or at least more interesting. Angels aren't bad of course. But if given the chance to see an angel or better understand Jesus, we should always choose Jesus.

Fourth is the ever-present temptation to reduce following Jesus to a list of regulations. This mentality says, "Don't drink, smoke, chew, or hang with others who do. And never, on any occasion, vote Democrat."[31] Some of

---

[30] Pliny the Elder, *Natural History*, 23.10.

[31] Or Republican, depending on what church you attend. ☺

these principles may indeed embody wisdom, but so often we (a) come up with our list of acceptable and unacceptable behaviors, (b) follow it to a tee, and (c) feel good about ourselves, whether or not we're actually loving God or people. Rules have their place and Paul isn't afraid to lay them down, but they can lead to a smug arrogance that hinders God's work in and through us. And we always have a tendency to create lists of rules that bear only glancing familiarity to the actual teachings and example of Jesus.

Paul's problem with all these things is that they represent paths toward growth that simply aren't the one God has chosen for us. Often they serve to work against their original intent of increasing our maturity. Most critically, they fail to magnify Jesus as the center of God's plan for transformation. Tomorrow, we'll begin unpacking just how this program works.

For now, consider yourself warned.

Framework
Chapter 23 – Colossians 3.1-4

My wife grew up in the tiny Midwest town of Leeton, MO, home to about 1000 people. We currently live in the northern reaches of Los Angeles County in Valencia, CA. Los Angeles and Leeton are about as different as two American cities can be. Let's pretend for a minute that life in Los Angeles is better than life in Leeton. And let's imagine we wanted to recreate in Leeton the life of L.A. What would we do?

We'd probably gather a collection of Angelinos, share our vision, and send them to Leeton to blaze the trail. First they'd be sure to purchase houses (or at least land) that cost twice as much as they could afford. Then they'd find jobs an hour-and-a-half away from where they live – you know, so they're never home to enjoy the houses they paid too much for. They'd start talking about the importance of organic food as if they invented the idea, which they'd ship in from far away while the local farmers look at them with understandable bewilderment. Of course they'd take their iPhones, and of course they'd never under any circumstances turn them off or leave them in another room. They'd text and email and surf the web before breakfast and on their lunch break and during dinner and any other time they're awake. They'd wear Lakers t-shirts when the Lakers are winning, don Dodgers hats when the Dodgers are winning, and fly Kings flags from their cars when the Kings are winning. (One guy would always wear his Clippers jersey, but even the Angelinos would look at him funny.)

I think you get the picture. Believe it or not, this hypothetical mission may help us understand the proper framework for growth in spiritual maturity. Jesus came from heaven to earth to live on earth the life of heaven – a life of complete trust in God and radical love for others. By his death and resurrection, Jesus made this same new life possible for all those in whom God's Spirit lives. As Paul writes elsewhere, because we are in Christ, we too have become part of God's mission of establishing and extending new creation within the old (2 Corinthians 5.17). We are transplants from another colony, sent from there to here to recreate here the life of there.

Let's map this out in picture form as a timeline. Many Jews of Jesus' day believed that when God sent the Messiah, he would usher in a new world that would replace the old one. Whereas the old world ruled by Sin is characterized by rebellion, anger, hatred, injustice, oppression, warfare, lust, and wrath, the new world ruled by God would overflow with love, forgiveness, justice, freedom, joy, and peace. Here is how they might have drawn history's timeline on a napkin:

They expected someone like Jesus to accomplish this decisive transformation in one blow. Jesus fulfilled their expectation about halfway. He inaugurated God's new world (as we learned back in week two), but he didn't completely do away with the old. The two "worlds" are now growing alongside one another, like this:

The life, death, and resurrection of Jesus generates the turn of the ages. The final truth to include is that God will one day finish what he started, that one day Jesus will return to bring full and final justice and restoration to our broken world. So our adjusted timeline now looks like this:

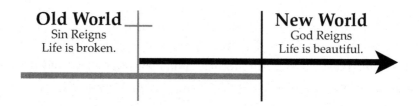

Notice the overlap between the first and second comings of Christ. This is where we currently live – in the time between the times. This contrast runs through all of Paul's writings and forms the backdrop for his program for spiritual growth. According to Paul, the tension between this present age and the age to come plays itself out in each of our lives. We have been called to live the life of God's promised future world – of "heaven," so to speak – in the midst of this present world on earth.

This is where the Los Angeles to Leeton analogy comes in. We are modeling a new way of life hoping others will see its value and embrace it as their own. Or to switch metaphors yet again, like a movie preview we give the rest of the world a glimpse of what is to come. Only in this case, the goal is not just that people will come see the movie, but that they'll actually join the cast. This is what following Jesus is all about. And this is why we feel pulled between good and evil, because both principles are at work in our world and our hearts.

Most of the time Paul writes about this conflict in terms of time. He talks about the "old" in contrast to the "new," as we saw in 2 Corinthians 5.17. But here in Colossians he changes the metaphor and explores the same realities using the language of space: below and above. (He probably does this to outflank the false teachers who made a big deal about ascendant heavenly visions.) Take a look at Colossians 3.1-4:

If, therefore, you were raised with Christ, seek the things above, where Christ is, where he is sitting at the right hand of God. Focus on things above, not on earthly things. For you died, and your life has been hidden with Christ in God. Whenever Christ – who is your life – is revealed, then you also will be revealed with him in glory.

Since we're changing metaphors, let's switch pictures as well. Instead of timelines, we'll use simple circles. Before Christ the world was ruled by darkness, but even then God's people received glimpses of a heavenly realm of life and light.

Once again, they expected that God would snap his powerful fingers and our dark world would immediately be replaced by a kingdom of light. But this is not what God did. Instead, in Christ God began invading this dark world below with the bright light from heaven above. As it stands, the two worlds overlap.

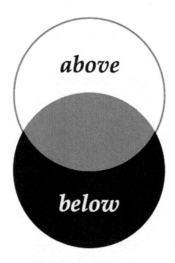

God completely reigns over heaven above – a realm where his will is perfectly and joyfully followed. And part of the universe continues in uninterrupted rebellion against that same will. But those who call Jesus Lord live and move in the grey overlap. God has transformed our minds and hearts so that we pursue good, but we are still susceptible to the seductions of evil.

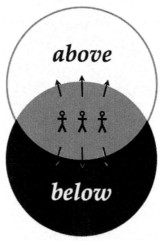

We are caught in the middle, called to live the life of God's new world while remaining in the brokenness of this one. The tension we feel as individuals between good and evil is part of a bigger cosmic conflict between creation and new creation, between God and Satan, between the life *above* and the life *below*. Throughout his letters, Paul finds no shortage of metaphors to describe how this battle plays out in our lives.

In Romans, Paul depicts this conflict as a literal war between "the Spirit" and "the flesh" (Romans 7.21-22, 8.5-6, 9). Paul enlists the same Spirit-flesh warfare metaphor in Galatians, and to it he adds the image of a tree bearing fruit (Galatians 6.16-17, 19-23). In Philippians, Paul uses a political metaphor by referring to the church as a "colony of heaven" (1.20). Philippi sat near the site of a crucial battle in Roman history, after which it was given the status of "Roman colony" and became the home of many retired army veterans and other Roman citizens. The idea was that they would recreate the life of Rome there in Philippi. When Paul says "colony of heaven" he's not telling them to look forward to heaven in the future, but to recreate the life of heaven here and now. And in 2 Thessalonians 2.13, Paul makes the same point with the agricultural image of "firstfruits" – the first portion of a crop that tells you what the rest of the crop will look like.

In all these ways Paul teaches us the basic framework for our growth toward maturity in Christ. We are in the middle of a war between two worlds: old and new, flesh and Spirit, earthly and heavenly, below and above. We are called to live according to God's Spirit while remaining in a world still heavily influenced by the flesh – an *above* type of life in a *below* kind of world. This formed the basis for Paul's critique that we examined yesterday: Though "religious" in nature, those habits and practices are just another version of life from below. Here in Colossians 3 he will unpack the same realities with the metaphor of a new set of clothes, probably because Colossae had a thriving textile industry. We have taken off the Old garments that stink of corruption and clothed ourselves with the New.

We grow in Jesus not just so we can be good little boys and girls. We grow to witness to the fact that this tired and broken old world has been supplanted by a new one.

Secret
Chapter 24 – Colossians 3.1-4

I need to tell you a secret. I don't want to be dramatic, but I've got to be honest. This secret has the potential to change your life. Even if you already follow Jesus, chances are good that you've missed out on what might be the most important truth about spiritual life in Christ.

I realize I'm not the only one claiming to share life-transforming secrets. Some years back Rhonda Byrnes released a book called *The Secret* that spoke directly into the hopes of many in our culture. The book quickly became a bestseller and sparked something of a phenomenon centered on the law of attraction and the power of positive thinking. The basic idea is simple: Our thoughts influence our health and happiness. So if we learn to think only positive thoughts, this mental positivity will attract actual positivity. We will become healthier, happier, more productive, more successful people in every way.

The problem with *The Secret's* secret is that it isn't true.[32]

My secret is true. And it changes everything. What I need to tell you – what Paul everywhere assumes and here in Colossians 3 makes explicit – has two parts. There is a pre-secret and then the secret itself.

---

[32] Actually there are dozens of problems with *The Secret,* but all of them flow from the fact that it isn't true.

The pre-secret is that you and I share in the benefits of Jesus' victory over Satan and sin and death. This was a basic principle of ancient warfare. Whenever a king won a victory in battle, the entire kingdom tasted the benefits of that victory (at least in theory). We see this all over the Old Testament, not least in the life of King David. Numerous times David led his armies into war, and when he defeated Israel's enemies all Israel rejoiced. Why? Because his success meant an improved – or at least sustained – way of life for everyone. This cultural practice should help us understand Colossians 3.1-4:

If, therefore, you were raised with Christ, seek the things above, where Christ is, where he is sitting at the right hand of God. Focus on things above, not on earthly things. For you died, and your life has been hidden with Christ in God. Whenever Christ – who is your life – is revealed, then you also will be revealed with him in glory.

Notice that Paul tells us to concentrate on the things above, *where Christ is, where he is sitting at the right hand of God.* Paul is alluding to Psalm 110, the Old Testament passage most referenced in the New Testament. In Psalm 110, God issues King David an invitation: "Sit at my right hand until I make your enemies a footstool for your feet." In other words, come reign with me and watch as I extend your kingdom throughout all the earth. This is victory language, and here we find its deepest truth revealed in reference to Jesus. When Paul says to look upon Jesus sitting at God's right hand, he is reminding us of the victory Christ won on our behalf.

But Paul doesn't stop at *on our behalf.* The point isn't just that Christ has lived, died, and been raised again on our behalf. The point is that we have died and been raised *with him.* As we learned last week, through baptism we have been joined spirit-to-Spirit so that we actually taste the benefits of his reign. This is also precisely what we explored yesterday. The power of new creation has broken into the present in our own lives.

Like so many things Paul says, this is fantastic but difficult to grasp on the ground. What difference does it make? What does it really even mean?

Let's back up and get a running start. Yesterday we talked about how when we are joined with Christ, we become part of God's new creation. This framework further explains what we learned back in chapter 19 – that when we become followers of Jesus, God implants into our spirit a new kind of life that provides access to a whole new world of spiritual sustenance. As we learn to depend on and draw from this life implanted deep within our being, we become capable of doing what we could never do on our own. We become capable of living the life of God's new world while still existing with the parameters of this one. We become capable of authentic faith, radical hope, and miraculously selfless love.

What Paul says here pulls all this together: *Christ* literally *is your life.* Paul may very well have learned this concept from the Apostle John, who once wrote, "In him was life, and that life was the light of all mankind" (John 1.4). And again, "That which was from the beginning, which we have heard, which we have seen with our eyes, which we have looked at and our hands have touched — this we proclaim concerning the Word of life. The life appeared; we have seen it and testify to it, and we proclaim to you the eternal life, which was with the Father and has appeared to us" (1 John 1.1-2).

Jesus came to earth as the life of God incarnated as a human being. Jesus is the Spiritual life source God has planted deep within your soul.

Because we have been joined *with Christ* in death and resurrection – his physical, ours spiritual for now and physical later – he now lives *in us.* Maybe you noticed that when we discussed Colossians 2.27, I didn't fully explain how Paul defined *the glorious riches of this mystery.* Do you remember what he said? This rich mystery is nothing less than *Christ in you.*

Jesus Christ is living the Christian life in you. This is the secret that changes everything.

Imagine a man trying to start a car with no gasoline. Picture a woman sitting at her desk punching away on a keyboard attached to a computer that isn't plugged in. Envision a young family gathered around the television for some quality time playing video games, only they're holding cordless controllers that have no batteries.

There's a decent chance all these scenarios are metaphors for you. If you've been relying on your own resources, there is more than just a chance. You have been attempting to do something impossible. You have been trying to obey Jesus on your own. It's not working, is it?

You don't have to live this way anymore. You need only rely on the life source that has already been planted in you. Simply take advantage of what you've already been given access to. Don't burden yourself with the pressure to manufacture spiritual life on your own. Jesus is living his life in you. Or at least he's trying to. All you have to do is give him space to operate. All you have to do is surrender to the One whose Spirit now dwells within you.

This concept came together for me during a conversation with my friend Dan. Dan is a gifted musician. He has a rare combination of talents in that he can not only play and sing, but also write both excellent lyrics and quality music. I was asking him how much of this process is pure creativity and how much is more scientific in nature. He answered by explaining how the right (creative) and left (logical) sides of his brain work together when he writes music and lyrics. The process usually begins with some sort of inspiration. This could come from literally anywhere – a tree, a sermon, traffic. An idea, a story, or an image just sort of grabs you. Then there is definitely a logical aspect to it – switching one phrase or chord combo for another to make the most beautiful sound possible. But at a certain point, you basically turn off your left brain as much as possible so the right brain can dance freely. Then you turn the left back on to organize the finishing touches. Roughly speaking, the right brain produces the power of new musical life, which the left brain first submits to and then structures into something beautiful and specific.

Maybe it's a rough analogy, but consider the parallels. Christ comes to us first and grabs hold of our heart or mind, at which point we say yes and open ourselves up to journeying with him. God implants the life of Christ in us through his Spirit, which provides the raw materials and power to live differently. Then we surrender ourselves to this newly implanted source of life. As we allow this indwelling Life to guide and shape our priorities and desires and habits, our hearts are transformed so that we actually see what Christ sees, want what he wants, trust like he trusts, and love like he loves. The result is that you come to naturally think more like Jesus and therefore live more like Jesus would if he were in your shoes.

We'll talk all week about how we actually fulfill our part of this cooperative affair, but if we begin with our effort then we will absolutely miss the freedom and joy God has in mind for us. We must first say with Paul, "I have been crucified with Christ and I no longer live, but Christ lives in me. The life I now live in the body, I live by faith in the Son of God, who loved me and gave himself for me" (Galatians 2.20).

The secret to "the Christian life" is that Jesus does the heavy lifting. He is the victorious King in whose triumph we participate. He is our indwelling

Lord to whom we joyfully surrender every moment of every day. He is our Power. He is our Sustenance. In a word, he is our Life.

Sin
Chapter 25 – Colossians 3.5-9

Sometimes sin doesn't seem that bad. "Sin" is such a menacing word, since, you know, it basically refers to the thing responsible for everything bad in our world. Sin names horrors like mass murder, corporate fraud, and child molestation. But sin also refers to telling white lies to get ahead in our careers, speaking to our spouses or children in a rude or demeaning tone, and not finding the right outlet for our anger. We wouldn't say these things are good, but they're just part of life. They can't be *that* bad, right?

Paul lists ten sins in Colossians 3, and if we're not careful we'll skip right over most of them, offering little more than a courtesy nod as we speed-read on to the positive stuff. Instead we need to camp out for a while so we understand what he says and why. Here is Colossians 3.5-9:

Put to death, therefore, the earthly parts: sexual immorality, impurity, impulsiveness, evil desires, and greed which is idolatry. Because of these God's wrath is coming. In them you too used to walk when you were living in these ways, but now also take off all such things as anger, rage, hatred, slander, and abusive words out of your mouth. Don't lie to one another, since you have stripped off the old humanity with its practices and have clothed yourself with the new.

For the second time in this letter, Paul talks directly about sin. Both times he drops a few hints that he's merely skimming the surface of much deeper realities. In 1.21 he says that our thoughts and deeds work together in a cyclical cause-and-effect way that ends with us being *alienated* from God and his will for our lives. And here in 3.5-9 he offers two lists of typical sins with a brief mention of idolatry and the wrath of God. When you follow the clues and consider what he says elsewhere, it becomes clear that Paul is writing about symptoms of a deep problem. Life has come alive in us, but death has not given up the fight.

Thankfully, what he alludes to here he fleshes out in more detail in the first few chapters of Romans. What I want to do is unpack what Paul says about sin in Colossians by examining Romans 1-3 alongside what the rest of the Scripture teaches about the process of sin ruining our lives, in particular the story of humanity's "fall" in Genesis 3. Stick with me because this might get a little heady, but understanding the way sin works will be worth it. So far as I can tell, we can break this descent down into five basic steps:

(1) *We refuse to trustfully acknowledge God as our king, and so we set up ourselves as competition.* This is clearly the issue in Genesis 3 – we want to be like God, knowing everything he knows. We reject the offer of ruling on his behalf, preferring to become kings and queens in our own right. Or as Paul says in Romans 1, we refuse to thank God and glorify him as God. Our refusal feeds off our fear that God cannot be trusted, that he doesn't have our best interests in mind. We question his love and assume he's holding out on us. I'd call this first step *rebellion*.

(2) *We assign sacredness to some other group* (our team, family, country, clique) *or symbolic object* (the sun, a flag, a clothing brand, dollar bills) *or idea* (liberty, happiness, art, socialism, capitalism, religion). We treat this thing like God, offering our support and looking to receive from it life and meaning and security. At this point, we are still in control (or so we think), freely choosing what to value or devote ourselves to. But we are treating as ultimate something other than God. This is again what Paul talks about in Romans 1, echoing the mocking of human-made idols we see all over the prophets (Isaiah 44.9-20; Psalm 115.1-8). This second step I'd specifically call *idolatry*.

(3) *We become like what we "worship" and so spiral downward into something less than what we were designed to be.* One of the basic biblical truths about worship is that we end up looking like what we make ultimate in our lives

136

(2 Kings 17.15; Psalm 115.8; Jeremiah 2.5; Hosea 9.10). Again this is part of what Paul is describing in Romans 1 – we trade in lives and a world made in God's image for lives and a world made in the image of something much smaller, so our humanity shrinks. We become less human and more beast-like, tearing one another apart at the seams. Witness Genesis 4-11, for example, or Romans 1.29-31. I'd call this step *corruption*.

(4) *We find ourselves controlled by the system, unable to break free from the huge suicide machine we've constructed.* Think about the problem of corporate greed, neglect of the poor, or abuse of the environment. These things are inescapably sinful, but the people making the harmful decisions often feel like they have no decision at all. They feel trapped by their history, by a competitive market, by an unaware public, and so on. The same is true in families. Marriages spiral downward until spouses have forgotten how to show love even when they want to, and they're afraid to want to because their efforts might not be reciprocated. This is the enslavement described in John 8, Romans 6, Titus 3, etc. I'd call this stage *bondage*.

(5) *We resign ourselves to despair, believing the lie that our dungeon is actually paradise, or the lie that though it is indeed a dungeon there's nothing we can do about it.* There are two tracks this can take. One is that we end up "calling evil good" as Paul talked about in Romans 1. We accept a purposeless existence in which anything goes. Of course this only makes the problem worse, but who cares, right? Or the second track is that we see problems – in our world, our communities, our families, and our hearts – and feel totally helpless to solve them. So we give up and settle for a decent existence with an adequate house, 2.5 kids, a car that runs, and maybe a few church or humanitarian donations to ease our conscience. I'd call this step *depravity* or *despair*.

So the spiral downward begins with rebellion and moves through idolatry to corruption, bondage, and depravity or despair. I really do believe that this provides a solid base from which we could understand everything happening in our world. And I believe it provides the necessary backdrop for Paul's sin lists in Colossians 3.

But of course Paul doesn't say all of this here in Colossians. To stay with his clothing metaphor, he doesn't detail the process of shopping or getting dressed. He just looks at the old life, sees folks walking around in body bags, and acknowledges that this cannot possibly be the best available apparel. So like a friend thoughtful enough to say, "Um, you really *shouldn't* wear that out of the house, or even in the house for that matter," Paul names for us ten of the specific items we must avoid.

Paul divides his list into two groups of five, each with a particular theme. The first five focus on sins of desire with an emphasis on sexual deviance. *Sexual immorality* heads the list as a general term for any sexual activity outside the context of husband-and-wife marriage. *Impurity* is also a general term for acting without wholesome intentions. *Impulsiveness* stands at the center and speaks of the attitude that says, "I'm going to let my desires be my guide and do what I want." We follow our emotions and intuitions, which spring from *evil desires* more often than we admit. Surprisingly, this first half is rounded out by the sin of *greed*. Paul sees quite well that the deformed desire for more lies at the root of much of our problems, sexual and otherwise. Notice how he even identifies greed with idolatry, which as we noted above is a major step toward human corruption. In the absence of other gods, we assume the throne ourselves.

The second half focuses on sins of anger with an emphasis on speech. *Anger, rage,* and *hatred* refer to different degrees of wishing ill will on other people. At times our anger manifests itself in physical attack, but more often we choose socially safer forms of violence like *slandering* people's character and even outright *abusing* them with our *words*. In some ways Paul's lists work together: We desire certain things out of life so we follow our hearts and pursue them; when our wants are halted we get angry, which often results in us tearing other people down with our mouths.

Paul says these patterns of living stand under God's judgment as expressions of and pathways toward his wrath, and he insists that God has freed us from the bondage they represent. What should we do in response? *Take off all such things.* Like a filthy stained shirt, strip off the old way of life and throw it in the trash. And as if to reinforce and even strengthen his point, *put* these things *to death*. Clearly Paul sees even small sins as requiring a serious response.

The last thing to notice is the way Paul holds together what we so often separate. Some of us faithfully uphold God's bans against sexual sin, but we do so in a manner marked by anger and condescension toward those who don't follow suit. Others among us avoid anger and meanness but fail to maintain other moral boundaries God has placed around our lives. Each side judges the other's sin as worse. But the point is not to choose some sins as "extra bad" and then pretend we're good for avoiding them. The point is to become aware of and take seriously the different ways we are pulled away from the life God designed for us. And as for which sin is worse, the best answer I've heard is, "The one you're about to commit."

Renewal

Chapter 26 – Colossians 3.10

We all refuse to allow certain things to happen to us. One of my friends grew up dirt poor and spent much of his childhood living in a car. He refuses to allow the same tragedy to overtake his family. My wife and I grew up in loving but broken homes, and we refuse to allow the same history of divorce to become our story. Some people refuse to let their bodies get out of shape, so they eat right and exercise religiously. Others refuse to be hurt emotionally, which generally means they're either very picky about who they love or they decide not to risk love at all. Still others, such as great athletes or successful businessmen, refuse to lose. We can't always control all the factors and we don't always get our way, but we all refuse to allow certain things to happen in our lives. We should reflect intentionally about our own refusals because they provide a clear window into what matters most to us.

What if we refused to dishonor Jesus? What if we not only added this to our list of refusals, but put it at the top where it belongs? What if we decided on pain of death that under no circumstances would we ever knowingly allow ourselves to act in ways that would not please Jesus?

As we've seen, Jesus calls for precisely this level of commitment:

If you want to be my disciple, you must deny yourself, take up your cross daily and follow me. For whoever wants to save their life will lose it, but whoever loses their life for me and for the gospel will save it.

If anyone comes to me and does not hate father and mother, wife and children, brothers and sisters—yes, even their own life—such a person cannot be my disciple.

Anyone who loves their father or mother more than me is not worthy of me; anyone who loves their son or daughter more than me is not worthy of me.

What would happen if we did what he's asking? What would change if we took off our body bags once and for all? How would our lives and our world look if all who claimed the name "Christian" or "follower of Jesus" absolutely refused to tolerate disobedience to Jesus in their own lives? Would we finally defeat the one sin that still has a grip in our hearts? Would we become better husbands and wives, mothers and fathers? Would we approach our 9-to-5 with a different mindset? Would we think different thoughts about the person in the cubicle next to us or in traffic alongside us? Would we eat or drink or spend our vacations differently than we do now? Would we change the world? What would happen if we refused to be unfaithful to Jesus?

The sad thing is that we might never find out.

I know one thing you can count on: We'll never come close to this kind of devotion unless we understand *why*.

In the book *Start With Why*, motivation specialist Simon Sinek argues that the most important question for any person or company is not "What are we going to do?" but "Why do we exist?" When we start with What, we eventually burn out because we forget the reasons we started in the first place. When we start with Why, we're prepared for anything. He credits the success of companies like Apple or Southwest Airlines not to what they do but to their painstaking clarity on why they do it.

Consider the more down-to-earth example of two construction workers. You approach the first and ask him if he likes his job. "I've been doing the same thing every day for as long as I can remember," he replies. "This wall is ridiculously large, my materials are heavy, the sun is hot, I work long hours, and I don't even know if we'll be done before I retire." You move to another section of the building and ask the second man the same question.

"I love what I do. We're building a cathedral where people from all over the world will come in search of God. The work is hard, we've been at it for a while, and I have no idea when we'll actually finish, but we're building a church. What else could I ask for?" One of these two men knows his *why*. When you know your why, you'll do whatever is necessary to get the job done.[33]

In some ways, Paul has been answering the why question throughout Colossians 3. He offers three basic answers, relating to our past, present, and future respectively. Let's work backwards and remember what he has said.

As we learned in chapter 22, Paul places our spiritual growth within the framework of the world *below* versus the world *above*, which is a reworking of his typical contrast between old and new. Basically, he tells us that when we obediently follow Jesus we are previewing our ultimate future. We become a faithful sign and foretaste of the age to come. It's like when a baseball prospect gets called up to the big leagues for a few weeks to give him a taste of what's to come. We are becoming the people we will be for all eternity. God's future for the world is breaking into the present in our own hearts and lives.

As for the present, in chapter 23 we learned that when we direct ourselves toward the life from above, we are stepping in line with what God is already doing. It's like joining the winning team or the company on the rise. This is what God is doing right now, and he has invited us to play our part.

Why go all in with Jesus? First, because we are anticipating our ultimate destiny. Second, because we are partnering with what God is actively doing today. And now Paul adds a third reason: because in Christ we are achieving our original purpose. You might have missed this point because it's tucked away in the last half of verse 10: *Don't lie to one another, since you have stripped off the old humanity with its practices and have clothed yourself with the new, **which is being renewed in knowledge according to the image of its Creator**.*

Do you ever have those moments when you just *know* that you're doing what you were meant to do? (Think Eric Liddell in *Chariots of Fire*, "When I run, I feel his pleasure.") It could be running or teaching or writing or performing brain surgery. Maybe you felt this way on your wedding day or

---

[33] Simon Sinek, *Start With Why* (London: Penguin, 2009), 34-35.

the moment your child was born or your first day on the job. Those brief instants when you feel connected to the core of your being, when you realize that if life is a road you're definitely headed in the right direction. Sometimes life just fits and you feel in a very deep sense that you are finding your home in this universe.

Whether you psychosomatically *feel* this or not, when you follow Jesus you are literally achieving the purpose for which you were designed. You are, as one teacher put it, "working with the grain of the universe."[34] In this pursuit you are like a plane flying, a flower blooming, a linebacker tackling, a meal satisfying, or a fan blowing cool air. Simply put, human beings were programmed to look like Jesus. You were created to live like Jesus would if he were in your shoes.

Paul communicates this truth by using creation language. Words like *knowledge, image, and creator* recall Genesis 1-3. God *created* humans *in his image* to rule on his behalf, but we wanted God's *knowledge* for ourselves so we revolted. Also remember anytime Paul uses *image* in this way he's referring to the fact that Jesus came and accomplished that original purpose of ruling on God's behalf. Where we failed, Jesus succeeded. Here in Colossians 3, Paul takes it a step further and teaches that as we follow Jesus, we participate in his success. We are stepping into the clothes we were designed to wear. God's original intentions for us are being *renewed*.

Sometimes people criticize Christianity because it isn't the "oldest" religion. Judaism is a couple millennia older, and eastern religions like Buddhism or Hinduism precede it by at least a few hundred years. But this entire argument is based on the mistaken idea that "Christianity" began in the first century AD. On the contrary, what we have come to know as "Christianity" – the life of Christ flowing through us as we ourselves follow the teachings and example of the Image of the Invisible God – has been around since the beginning. The one we've come to know as Jesus Christ was the original template for humankind. So as you follow him – as you grow in the kind of maturity he defines and empowers – remember that you are becoming nothing less than what God envisioned at the beginning. This is your why. This is your destiny.

---

[34] This phrase first appeared in John Howard Yoder's "Armaments and Eschatology" in *Studies in Christian Ethics* 1, no 1 (1988), 58). The full sentence reads, "People who bear crosses are working with the grain of the universe."

Interference
Chapter 27 – Colossians 3.11

Back in junior high my friends and I got busted for "gang-related activity." The school called in a local gang task force officer who threatened to classify us all as gangsters downtown so that anytime someone pulled our record, they would know the (supposed) truth about our past. I don't remember the name of our gang, but my nickname was "White." (Many things we enjoyed in abundance, but creativity wasn't one of them.) I don't mean to make light of gangs – most are tragic in the deepest ways – but ours was amusingly un-dangerous. We weren't really a gang. We were just a group of friends having a little fun and carving out for ourselves a shared sense of identity and togetherness.

Your whole life you've belonged to groups. They may have been violent or peaceful groups, cool or lame groups, rich or poor groups, smart or dumb groups, joyful or bitter groups, trendy or fringe groups, black, white, or colorful groups, athletic, intellectual, or musical groups. Nations. Tribes. Fan clubs. Bands. Posses. Staffs. Crews. Religions.

We group up with others who look like us or have the same skill sets or hobbies or convictions. If you're a scrapbooker, you scrapbook with other scrapbookers. If you're an athlete, you form teams with other athletes. People who love motorcycles hang with other people who love motorcycles. Same goes for singles and married couples, parents and non-parents, coffee, baking, politics, or beer. If you're a liberal or conservative, most of your close friends probably are too. If you only drink Guinness, chances are your besties don't prefer Bud Light. Even if you're a loner there's a certain group identity that binds you together with all those other people who choose against friendship. We associate with many groups almost every day, some of which stand in competition with one another. Management or Labor? Mac or PC? Red Sox or Yankees?

Colossians 3.11 comes out of nowhere.

Paul's argument is moving along quite nicely. This is actually most people's favorite portion of the letter, because we love hearing Paul describe the process of transformation that God is working in our lives. And then all of a sudden he throws in a line about groups: *Here there is no Greek and Jew, circumcision and uncircumcision, foreigner, savage, slave, or free, but Christ is all and in all.* This is hardly the only time Paul says something like this. Here are a couple other examples: "There is neither Jew nor Gentile, neither slave nor free, nor is there male and female, for you are all one in Christ Jesus" (Galatians 3.28). "For we were all baptized by one Spirit so as to form one body – whether Jews or Gentiles, slave or free – and we were all given the one Spirit to drink" (1 Corinthians 12.13).

Clearly Paul considers this an important point. But here in Colossians it comes out of left field. Or to switch sports metaphors, if Paul's letter is a wide receiver running across the field to catch a pass, then this line is a cornerback who appears from nowhere and lays the receiver out before the ball arrives. This is called pass *interference*. Matter of fact, interference is precisely Paul's point.

Like you and I, the Colossians lived in a fragmented world – haves and have nots, natives and foreigners, that sort of thing. And like us, these folks belonged to many of those groups. Groups hold a special place in our hearts, which is – or at least may be – precisely the problem. You need to understand this if you want to live in ways that please God. You must get this if you don't want to work against the life that Jesus is living in and through you. The groups you belong to may interfere with your obedience to God. Past and present group identities and allegiances pose a threat to faithfully following Jesus.

There are two basic reasons for this. The first is simply that many groups form our hearts around goals and values that conflict with the way of Jesus. Consider the Ku Klux Klan as an obvious and extreme example: You cannot remain committed to Ku Klux Klan ideals and faithfully follow

Jesus. Most groups are more subtle, of course, which is why we must always be on guard against trying to fit Jesus into some other mold.

The second is that we internalize our group alliances so that they become part of our core identity. This comes out most clearly in how we treat opposing groups. For example, consider college sports allegiances. In 2012 the NCAA Basketball Final Four featured two Kentucky teams separated by less than eighty miles: the Cardinals from Louisville and the UK Wildcats from Lexington. The week before the game, a few folks were predicting outcomes at a dialysis clinic. A man named Charles was waiting in line and bragging to another patient about the University of Louisville. University of Kentucky fan Ed inserted himself into the conversation while undergoing treatment, and apparently told Charles to shut up. He added a finger gesture for good measure. So what did Charles do next? He walked up to Ed *and punched him in the face!* We're talking about grown men coming to blows over college allegiances *in a dialysis clinic.*[35] Sometimes nothing will stop us from standing up for our group.

With all this in mind, let's dig a bit more into Colossians 3.11: *Here there is no Greek and Jew, circumcision and uncircumcision, foreigner, savage, slave, or free, but Christ is all and in all.* Notice the different types of groupings Paul targets. First he goes after our ethnic or national group identities. For Jews there were two kinds of people: Jews and non-Jews. Often we find the general word "Gentiles" which is actually the word *ethnē* in Greek and can be translated "nations." Here Paul uses the more specific label "Greek," but it basically means the same thing.

Let's be as clear as possible on what this means. Racism has absolutely no place in the church. You cannot follow Jesus faithfully and consider folks of another race inferior or by definition less moral or wise. Nationalism has no place in the church. The church is an international or multinational community, and to allow our more tightly defined national identities – American, Italian, South African, etc – to eclipse our identity as Christians is below the line of acceptability. We can by all means love and appreciate our countries, and we'd be fools to act like all nations are equal in every way. But we are Jesus-followers first, and only secondly Canadians or Japanese or whatever.

---

[35] See the story at http://www.courier-journal.com/article/20120327/SPORTS13/303270063/fight-at-dialsys-center. Accessed 6/27/12.

Second, Paul refers to religious group identities. Specifically, Paul is talking about different groups within the church – Jewish Christians and Gentile Christians. The primary conflict within the first century church was between these two factions. At times each one sought to establish superiority over the other, and more than one of Paul's letters attack precisely this problem. We don't have to think hard to find modern parallels. We have Baptists, Presbyterians, Methodists, Nazarenes, Catholics, non-denominationals, and hundreds of others. Denominations aren't going away anytime soon, so our task today is to refuse to allow our particular brands of church or theology to call into question the legitimacy of others who believe in and follow Jesus as Savior and Lord.

Paul's next terms encompass a few kinds of groups: political, cultural, and linguistic. Often the three are mashed together. While Jews divided the world into Jews and Gentiles or Greeks, Greeks often divided the world between Greeks and "Barbarians," which meant anyone who didn't speak Greek. *Foreigners* is the word I've gone with, though we could just as easily use *immigrants* or *refugees*. And if you don't think language is still a barrier in this regard, think about how many times you've heard something like this, "If *they* want to come to *our* land, *they* should learn to speak *our* language." Think what you want politically, but that kind of attitude has no place among those who know that Christ is all and in all.

After *foreigners* Paul mentions "Scythians," who were the farthest reaches of barbarians – *savages* known for their crudity, excess, and harsh ways of living. We're talking about cultural distinctions at their finest, like the tension felt when someone from rural Arkansas visits New York City, or when San Franciscans travel to middle Montana. Thankfully, the church is big enough for all of us. We might find each other exceedingly odd, but we cannot forget that in the church we are nevertheless brothers and sisters.

The last division Paul mentions is both social and economic. Here there is neither *slave* nor *free*. We'll talk more about masters and slaves next week, but for now let's acknowledge that breaking down group barriers doesn't get any more radical than this!

We are part of a *new humanity*. A new centrally defining group. A community that welcomes with open arms people of every race, country, denomination, party, heritage, language, class, and status. Here in this new humanity all old allegiances are relegated to a distant second place by our shared love for and allegiance to Christ, who *is all and in all.*

Dream

Chapter 28 – Colossians 3.12-14

Transformation begins in the imagination. Michael Jordan believed he would become Michael Jordan before any of us knew his name. America began as an idea that just enough people believed in just enough to make it happen. Sam Walton envisioned a buy-everything-here chain of stories long before Walmart forever imprinted the world of retail. Some kid is walking around knowing he (or she) will one day be elected the 52nd President of the United States. You have to see something before you'll take the necessary steps to become something.

At the corner of the highest point in the city of Athens, Greece, sits a flagpole. Currently the blue-and-white Greek flag flies proudly, but this was not always the case. During the dark days of WWII, Nazis replaced the Greek flag with their own. It may seem like a small move, but for the citizens below who woke up each day to that red and white fabric flapping in place of their beautiful blue, the symbolism was undeniable. The Nazis now ruled their world. Then one night some young idealists climbed to the top and returned the Greek flag to its rightful place. The next morning the city awoke to shouts of joy as all the citizens assumed the war was over and their homeland was returned to order. Their celebration proved premature, of course, for nothing substantial had changed since they went to bed the night before. But even after those in power re-raised their red flag by full sunrise, the damage was done. The hour or two of jubilation ignited a Greek revolution that ended with them ousting the powerful Nazi regime not too long thereafter. Transformation begins in the imagination.

Truth be told, all human change follows the same basic pattern. We become inspired by a new vision of what our lives could become, often in very specific ways. The new picture drives us to commit ourselves to whatever course of action is necessary to turn our dream into reality. Then we do just that, employing whatever means and methods are required. A classic example is learning a new language. No one learns a new language until they've caught a glimpse of how their life would be enhanced or improved by knowing how to speak Spanish or Cantonese or French. Whether we're missionaries, business executives, history buffs, or people who want to sound romantic, we imagine the new possibilities so vividly that we decide the work will be worth the reward. At that point we make the crucial decision to commit to learning the language, after which we may buy books, listen to audio tracks, perhaps even spend some time in another country.

Notice the pattern. First, our imaginations are ignited by a compelling glimpse of our lives after the change. Second, we commit ourselves to the process of transformation. Third, we seek out and stick with the means of getting there. For our purposes today, focus on the beginning of the process. Transformation begins in the imagination.

Over the next few days, Paul will paint for us a vision of this life *from above* that he holds in such high regard. Use your imagination and see what your life and your church can look like, he says, if you create enough room for God to do what he wants – if you focus on the life from above and put to death what doesn't align. Let's start with Colossians 3.12-13:

> *Clothe yourselves, therefore, as God's chosen people, set apart and loved, with genuine compassion, kindness, humility, gentleness, and patience, bearing with one another and graciously forgiving each other if anyone has a complaint against another. Just as the Lord graciously forgave you, you do the same.*

Linger for a while, because this is more than just a list. It's a vision. It's a dream. Imagine how your life might be different if you become the kind of person God dreamt of when he saved you. And don't just stop with your own life. Many of our churches are known for being judgmental, anti-gay,

149

and pawns of political power. How might the world might change if our churches instead become known for *genuine compassion, kindness, humility, gentleness, and patience*?

Without sanding down the collective impact of this list, let's dig a little into the specific aspects of Paul's description. Notice, first, that it begins with God's love as the defining mark of our identity. Who are we? We are the people God dearly loves, those he has chosen out of the world as his special possession and set apart to help continue his mission. This love is not something that comes and goes when there's company coming around. It is a love we did not earn and therefore cannot lose. We can do nothing to make God love us any more and nothing to make God love us any less. This fact alone explains the other qualities Paul mentions, for they are but reflections of this love mirrored outward.

From this foundation Paul builds a structure to display this reflected love. Paul begins with *genuine compassion*, which comes from the word for bowels or guts. In a world grown cold to human suffering, we are a people who cannot see other people hurting without sharing their pain deep in our souls. This isn't just a compassion that leads to tears, but rather to help. Of course *kindness* includes not being mean, but niceness is hardly the whole of it. Kindness means doing what we can to help those for whom we feel compassion: encouraging the depressed, listening to the ignored, providing for those without basic resources.

In all this we enact *humility*. Contrary to popular opinion, humility is not about thinking we are lame or worthless. Humility begins by thinking rightly of ourselves – though wonderfully made, we are nonetheless made. We are not God. And knowing ourselves to be well-loved non-gods, humility also includes the next step of not thinking about ourselves at all. We come to see our lives as a gift God wants to use to bless others, so we take the focus off me. No one is beneath our time or attention. No one is too dirty or poor or lowly to merit our help.

Knowing we are not God, we don't fly off the handle in anger when we don't get our way. Matter of fact, as we allow the life of Jesus to flow through us, we react to slight or offense with measured *gentleness*. When you respond to someone harshly you act as if the world is a kingdom and you are royalty. How dare you say or do that to *me*? The opposite isn't to see yourself as nothing and let everyone trample on you, but rather to gently expose wrongdoings with *patience*. Gentleness labels your approach:

strength under control rather than power gone wild. And patience describes how long this approach will last: as long as it takes.

In the ancient world, moral philosophers would often pile up virtues to paint a picture of the good life. So Paul's method here isn't odd. But the similarities die on the surface. Compassion? Gentleness? Humility? Typically these characteristics didn't qualify as virtues. Why? Because they were considered weak. But Paul doesn't care what the rest of the world thinks, because he's not describing *their* ideal. He's describing his. He's saying in detail what he puts more succinctly in Romans 13.14: "Clothe yourselves with Christ." Paul's dream centers thoroughly in Jesus, who once described himself as "gentle and humble in heart" (Matthew 11.30).[36]

Paul's vision paints a picture of the image God is transforming us into. We see here what we are becoming. Paul is describing the new outfit God is sewing around our skin. He portrays what the indwelling life of Christ looks like when it comes to fruition.

To add one more metaphor, Paul is defining what a "win" looks like for Jesus-followers. In business, wins are typically defined by profit margin and the bottom line. In family life, we win when our spouse feels supported and our kids know we love them. In sports, wins are defined by the scoreboard. In life with God, we win anytime we choose compassion over coldheartedness, kindness over inactivity, or humility over pride. When we stoop down and serve in ways we feel are beneath us, we are winning. When we resist the urge to blow up at our families or coworkers or fellow drivers, instead taking a deep breath and responding with gentleness and the long fuse of patience, we are winning. We are allowing the life of Christ to win over the power of our broken desires. We are manifesting the life of heaven on earth. We are saying yes to the life from above and no to the life from below. We are climbing into the clothes we were made to wear.

That's all fine and good, you might be thinking, but what do we do now? And the answer is that you become what you are becoming. Now that you've seen the destination, fall in line with what God is doing. Walk in the direction God is leading you. Turn this dream into reality, one small act of obedience at a time.

---

[36] We men in particular need to remember that Jesus of Nazareth – not William Wallace or James Bond or Michael Corleone – defines authentic manhood.

GROWTH

moreJESUS part 5 – COMMUNITY

In his bestselling book *Bowling Alone*, Harvard sociologist Robert Putnam analyzed loneliness and friendship in America. Among his most interesting findings was the connection between happiness, health, and community. One study found that people with more relationships get fewer colds. Apparently friendship actually stimulates our immune system. Another revealed that stroke victims with strong support networks functioned better after having a stroke. Putnam even discovered that people who are physically unhealthy but have meaningful relationships typically live longer than fit people with fewer friends.

Putnam concluded the following, "As a rough rule of thumb, if you belong to no groups but decide to join one, you cut your risk of dying over the next year in half."[37] Think about that for a minute. You can actually increase your years on earth by sharing your life with others.

This shouldn't surprise us. From the beginning of the Bible, God makes it clear that human beings were made to live in community. The first negative word God spoke over creation was, "It is not good for the man to be alone" (Genesis 2.18).[38] God's immediate answer was to create woman, so that together man and woman could populate the human family and overcome the problem of aloneness.

We are hardwired for community.

A northerner once traveled to the South and visited a local restaurant for breakfast. He saw grits on the menu but had no idea what that meant, so he asked the waitress, "What exactly is a grit?"

She responded as only a Southern waitress could, "Honey, they don't come by themselves."[39]

You and I are like grits. No grit is an island, and neither are we.

Our relational DNA bleeds through almost every page of the Bible's story. After the first family failed, God sought a new one – first Noah's, then

[37] Putnam, *Bowling Alone* (New York: Simon & Schuster), 331. Putnam reports on these and many other findings in Chapter 20, "Health and Happiness," pages 326-335.

[38] As a side note, one time I visited a church with Scripture verse references on various tiles of the bathroom floor. Right below the urinals you'll find none other than Genesis 2.18. Still true, but not exactly the best place for that particular reminder. I'm just saying.

[39] John Ortberg, *Everybody's Normal Till You Get to Know Them* (Grand Rapids: Zondervan, 2003), 18.

Abraham's. Abraham's family takes center stage in the biblical narrative, being chosen as God's appointed means of saving everyone else. We know the name Moses because he served as the liberator of an entire population from slavery. God spoke to him not for his own benefit but so that this holy nation could have laws to regulate their life together. Kings were called to serve the kingdom, and when they failed in this task God sent prophets to pronounce judgment – a judgment, not incidentally, that all Israel experienced together. Even Jesus didn't go it alone, instead calling together twelve leaders to represent the re-gathering of the ancient community of God (which had twelve tribes). This reconstituted family became the church, which means *us*. Indeed, we are who we are only in community.

From the cradle to the grave we reach out to be held, heard, touched, loved. But tragically, sometimes during the between years we stop reaching out. Some of us forget we were made for life together. Others don't forget so much as refuse to accept that we can't make it on our own. Still others – most of us, I'm guessing – simply become too ashamed or guarded or busy to let other people in.

Our isolationist tendencies are confirmed and fed by our surrounding culture, at least for those of us living in America. "Whether it is the penniless immigrant who became a self-made millionaire, the solitary cowboy riding out of Dodge City or the starving artist who defies convention, our folklore celebrates the individual who creates his or her own unique path."[40]

The problem isn't individuality, of course, but individualism: the belief (more often assumed than articulated) that I am the center of my universe.

We even bring this attitude to church. I grew up in a faith centered on the question, "Do you have a personal relationship with Jesus Christ?" It's by no means a horrible question, but it falls terribly short of encompassing all that God has in mind for his people.

Veteran pastor Eugene Peterson admits that even he took a while to learn this lesson: "I didn't come to the conviction easily, but finally there was no getting around it: there can be no maturity in the spiritual life, no obedience in following Jesus, no wholeness in the Christian life apart from an immersion and embrace of community. I am not myself by myself. Community, not the highly vaunted individualism of our culture, is the

---

[40] Steve Wilkens and Mark L. Sanford, *Hidden Worldviews* (Downers Grove: IVP, 2009), 28.

setting in which Christ is at play."[41]

In other words, for better or worse, more Jesus means more community. Which brings us back to Colossians 3. Paul doesn't stop talking about growth and start talking about community. More accurately, he simply can't explain the former without the latter. Growth in Christ by definition means growth as the church. And the church means neither you nor me but *us*. After solidifying this point by reexamining some of what we just studied, we're going to walk through Paul's description of life together. He begins with the church's way of handling conflict and moves quickly to the church gathered for worship. After a transitional reminder that neither worship nor the church is a part-time affair, he describes Jesus-followers at home and work.

Some of what Paul says might surprise you and other parts might shock or offend you, but all of it will make you think about what it means to live in community.

---

[41] Eugene Peterson, *Christ Plays in Ten Thousand Places* (Grand Rapids: Eerdmans, 2005), 226.

Together
Chapter 29 – Colossians 3.14

Have you ever wondered why you're so self-absorbed?

Probably not. Most of us drift through life never realizing how thoroughly self-centered we are. I'm not trying to be dramatic and I don't mean to say we *never* act outside of our own best interests. It's not that we don't care about other people at all. It's not that we're mean or stingy, unforgiving or disrespectful, too arrogant to associate with losers or too afraid to stick up for outsiders. I mean, don't get me wrong. We can all be uncaring, mean, stingy, unforgiving, disrespectful, arrogant, and cowardly. But the problem is much deeper than that.

Think about the word "self-absorbed." To absorb essentially means to take whatever is outside and draw it in. Sponges do this with water. Celebrities do this with attention. And again, most of us do this with, well, pretty much everything in our lives. We take what's out there – clothes, cars, successes, failures, people – and define them by how they impact what's in here. I'm not saying you're a mean girl or a bad dude, I'm just saying you're human. And being human in a world tainted by sin typically involves curving our entire world around our individual self. Everyone else becomes part of my story (or yours, as it were).

And herein lies the tragedy of human existence. From here flows the poison that corrupts bodies, souls, families, communities, nations, networks, corporations, ecosystems, and so on. The problem is that for the most part we measure everything with one thing in mind: me.

What do you think of your job or the people you work with? How is your marriage? Do you ever think about walking away? If you're single, who do you have your eyes on? Should you go back to school? How do you plan to spend your retirement? What do you think of all this God stuff anyway?

I have no idea precisely how you would answer these questions. But I know that if you're like me, you'll probably answer them by gauging how likely you are to get what you want. (Or resent the fact that you're no longer afforded that luxury.)

What *do* you want? Whether it's pleasure, joy, money, status, resolution, friendship, respect, security, trust, or peace of mind, we all want something. And what you want often becomes your measuring stick for, once again, pretty much everything.

Do you know the story of Narcissus? It's an ancient Greek myth about a hunter named Narcissus who was stunningly attractive. He was so self-absorbed that he found no one worthy of his affection. One day Nemesis showed Narcissus a pool where for the first time he saw his own reflection, and for the first time he finally fell in love – with himself! He was so taken with his own image (not realizing it wasn't a real person) that he refused to walk away from the beauty of his own reflection. Unable to leave the pool, he died.

The moral of the story is that if you focus too much on yourself, you'll wither up and die.

Truth be told, at some level we're all narcissists. What's more, we bring this deeply self-directed mentality into our faith. But unfortunately for us narcissists – or fortunately, I suppose, unless you want to die of self-absorption – Christianity is a team game. It's more basketball than golf, more marching band than solo guitarist, more movie script than monologue. This pilgrimage requires that we work together, value one another, and genuinely act with each other's interests in mind.

Today we're bringing above water an idea that has hidden just below the surface for the last few chapters – the unavoidably corporate nature of life and growth in Christ. Someone I love once said to me, "I can love Jesus without going to church." I don't think Paul would agree. For instance, did you notice how most of the sins Paul named were relational? *Sexual*

158

immorality and *impurity* almost always involve the breach of at least one human relationship. It doesn't take long to list entire families or companies that have been destroyed by one person's *impulsiveness*. *Greed* is often based on the comparison game: I want more than you have and you want more than I have, so together we spiral downward in an idiotic competition that serves no one. Greed is also a failure to use our resources to care for those in need. The second list is so thoroughly relational that no explanations are needed: *anger, rage, hatred, slander, abusive words,* and *lying*. All these are violations of genuine community, friendship, and love.

The same could be said of the virtues Paul mentions to describe our new clothing in Christ: *genuine compassion, kindness, humility, gentleness,* and *patience.* Remember also Paul's point that old group identities pose a significant threat to genuine growth in Christ.

But more than anything I want you to notice one word: love. *And over all these things put on* **love,** *which binds them together perfectly* (Colossians 3.14).

I'm not going to spend too much time defining love, because you already know what it is: prioritizing someone else's well-being above your own. My point is a little different, and it's anchored in the fact that Paul presents love as the epitome of renewed humanity in Christ. Here it is: If love is the epitome of renewed humanity, then renewed humanity is inescapably communal. If life in Christ is most clearly manifested in how you treat other people, then maturity is not something we can define by looking inward. Maturity manifests itself most clearly not in our personal "quiet times" with God – crucial as they may be – but in how we interact with our families, neighbors, coworkers, enemies, and friends.

Before I met my wife I considered becoming a monk. I know that's weird, but what can I say? The prospect of hanging out with God all day and not having to talk to anyone else had a certain appeal to me. Needless to say, I still had quite a bit to learn about Jesus. More Jesus means more church. More Jesus means more love. More Jesus means more community.

Think about it in reality television terms. Christianity is much more *Amazing Race* than *Survivor*. In *Survivor* other people exist for one purpose: to get me closer to a million dollars. At the end of the day, it doesn't matter if I like them, what tribe they're on, or even whether they're in my alliance. There is no real community in *Survivor*, because people essentially remain narcissistically focused on self. They work together and protect each other so long as doing so helps each individual win.

On the other hand, if you show up at the *Amazing Race* finish line alone, the contest is not over. You haven't won anything. This game is won or lost together. Life may often feel more like *Survivor*, but Christianity is more *Amazing Race*. This game is not something an individual can win.

Consider all the one another's we find in the New Testament. Colossians gives us *bearing with one another* and *graciously forgiving one another*, as well as *teach and admonish one another*. But this hardly cracks the surface. Others include the following:

Be devoted to one another in love. (Romans 12.10)
Honor one another above yourselves. (Romans 12.10)
Stop passing judgment on one another. (Romans 14.13)
Accept one another as Christ accepted you. (Romans 15.7)
Instruct one another. (Romans 15.14)
Serve one another humbly in love. (Galatians 5.13)
Carry one another's burdens (Galatians 6.2)
Be patient with one another. (Ephesians 4.2)
Be kind and compassionate to one another. (Ephesians 4.32)
Submit to one another out of reverence for Christ. (Ephesians 5.21)
Encourage one another and build one another up. (1 Thessalonians 5.11)
Spur one another on toward love and good deeds. (Hebrews 10.24)
Do not slander one another. (James 4.11)
Love one another deeply, from the heart. (1 Peter 1.22)
Clothe yourselves with humility toward one another. (1 Peter 5.5)
Greet one another with affection. (1 Peter 5.14)
Lay down our lives for one another. (1 John 3.16)
Take care of one another's material needs. (1 John 3.17-18)

Surely the point is clear. Following Jesus is about so much more than your own "personal relationship with God." It's a calling you cannot fulfill on your own, a journey we must take together.

Some folks in Colossians thought they had reached higher planes of spiritual living because they enjoyed thrilling experiences, followed stringent rules, and possessed special knowledge. They were wrong. Maturity is not defined by how much we know, but by how well we love. In the final analysis, how much you know does not matter, nor do all the delightful spiritual experiences you can recount or how many times you've been to church or how many rules you follow better than the person sitting next to you. If you treat other people poorly then you are not a mature follower of Jesus. If you subtly view other people as stepping stones to your own self-actualization – as bit parts of a story in which you're the star – then you need to grow up in Christ, get over yourself, and learn to love.

Conflict
Chapter 30 – Colossians 3.13-15

Many ideals are more often talked about than actually achieved. I know lots of people who say they will someday climb a mountain, run a marathon, backpack through Europe, quit an addiction, start a business, write a book, or learn how to love their families.

And I know more than a few people who talk more than a little about community.

But the problem is community kind of burns sometimes. Henri Nouwen once famously said that community is the place where the person you least want to be around lives. Or as Eugene Peterson colorfully puts it, "Jesus doesn't seem to be very discriminating in the children he lets into his kitchen to help with the cooking." [42] More simply, the problem with community is that it's full of people.

Selfish people. Malicious people. Deceitful people. Unforgiving people. Abrasive people. Shy people. Mean people. Negative people. People with bad attitudes. Opinionated people. Liberals. Conservatives. Sinners. Saints. (Difficult to say which is worse.) People who talk so quiet you can't hear what they're saying. People who talk so loud you can't hear what you're thinking. People who make more money than you and enjoy bigger homes, better vacations, and nicer (or at least safer!) cars. People who don't make

---

[42] Peterson, *Christ Plays*, 226.

any money and want to borrow some of yours. People less intelligent than you who can't seem to get it. People more intelligent than you who look at you like you don't get it. People who smoke. People who drink. People who swear. People who wouldn't be caught dead smoking, drinking, or swearing. People who abuse. People who let people abuse.

You know what I mean? I mean, don't get me wrong. I love people. But we're kind of a mess. People are fickle, arrogant, unreliable, violent, unstable, and stinky. So am I. So are you. And yet community can't happen without us. Worse yet, community can't happen without *them*.

All this results in a predictable proverb: with community comes conflict. Every time.

Matter of fact, you can't have authentic community without conflict. Does that surprise you? We don't typically evaluate our relationships this way. If someone asked if your family or workplace had experienced significant conflict in the past six months and you said yes, you wouldn't be bragging. Nonetheless, conflict will come and it provides all kinds of good opportunities. We'll consider some of those opportunities – and better understand why the presence of conflict can be good news – a bit later. First let's reflect on how the Bible says to engage conflict.

The Bible is pretty clear about the general logistics. If you have something against someone, go to that person directly and seek restoration. If you two can't work it out, bring in others to help mediate the situation (or confront the sin). If that doesn't work, call in some leaders within your church community to help you come to an agreement, peacefully agree to disagree, or discern what other steps need to be taken.

It's not rocket science, which may be why Paul tends to emphasize not the logistics of conflict but the spirit of conflict – the attitude and approach we need in order to do conflict well. In Galatians he mentions dealing with conflict created by someone's sin, and his main point is that you should seek restoration *gently* (6.2). Dealing with a similar situation in 1 and 2 Corinthians, he does present a resolution process but he also emphasizes the purposes and tone necessary for things to work. In Philippians he actually calls out two women (Euodia and Syntoche) and tells them to agree with each other, which builds on what he had just written about having the same selfless attitude of Jesus (Philippians 2.1.11).

What Paul says about conflict in Colossians builds on and blends with what we've just explored, so I'll highlight the specific parts we're concentrating on today.

Clothe yourselves, therefore, as God's chosen people, set apart and loved, with genuine compassion, kindness, humility, gentleness, and patience, **bearing with one another and graciously forgiving each other if anyone has a complaint against another. Just as the Lord graciously forgave you, you do the same.** *And over all these things put on love, which binds them together perfectly.* **And let the peace of Christ arbitrate in your hearts; into this peace you were called in one body.**

Paul highlights three aspects of a Jesus-centered loving approach to conflict. First, this spirit of conflict builds on one of the most important "one another's" we find in the Bible – *bearing with one another.* This is a constant and necessary step in forming community, because we are constantly tempted to give up on each other. When relationships get rough, we want to move on. We write each other off and get on with our lives. But to *bear with one another* means we stay put rather than running away. Jesus-followers are not people who do nothing wrong. Rather, we are people who don't give up on each other when wrong is done. We put up with one another. We share our burdens. We engage rather than letting everyone go their own way.

The fact that we bear with one another leads us into conflict rather than away from it, and what Paul says next describes what we do once we get there: *graciously forgiving each other if anyone has a complaint against another.* Paul doesn't use the normal word for forgiveness here, which speaks about no longer holding people's wrongs against them. Instead Paul uses a word that emphasizes the graciousness of forgiveness – the fact that forgiveness gives people better than what they deserve. We offer forgiveness even when people haven't earned it – even when they've earned the opposite. Why? Because we are reflecting toward others the same forgiveness the Lord has shown us.

We'd be wise to pause at this point and remember that we're not studying Colossians just to understand what Paul said. Our goal is to let God work in us the same way he worked in them. With that in mind, I need to ask you a couple questions. First question: Whom in your life do you need to forgive? Whether it's a huge offense or just a minor infraction, you still harbor negative thoughts toward someone for what they've done. You need to go to that person and tell them what they've done wrong (as gently as you can). Don't say, "It's okay" or "Water under the bridge." Forgiveness begins not by downplaying how we've been hurt but facing what's been done in all it's wrongness. And then – when the wrong has been named and identified as not okay – offer that person forgiveness. They may reject you or deny what they did or tell you to get over it. They may even laugh at you. That's not on you. What's on you is to offer forgiveness to those who have wronged you.

Second question: Whose forgiveness do you need to seek? Who have you wronged that you must go to, admit the truth, and ask for forgiveness? They may flip out when they discover what you've done. Or they may ridicule you for making a big deal out of something small. That's not on you. What's on you is to seek forgiveness from those you've wronged.

Jesus actually says elsewhere that if while worshiping God you remember an unresolved conflict between you and another Jesus-follower, then you need to stop worshiping, go to that person, and make things right. If this is you, please put this book down and go to that person and begin or continue the process of reconciliation. If you can't physically go to them, make a phone call or write a letter. If they've passed away, write the letter you'd give them if they were still around. And share these experiences with others who can encourage you and help you work toward healing.

And as you go (or now that you're back), remember what Paul offers as the foundation for this entire process: *the peace of Christ*, into which we *were called in one body*. What does Paul mean by this? He means that we've been united as a community in spite of our differences. Our unity doesn't depend on having the same opinions or preferences or styles. Our commonality is Christ. He is the peace that holds us together. We must allow this peace to be the referee or arbitrator as we work through conflict with one another. We allow our unity in Christ to trump whatever differences or grievances we have with each other.

Most people take a "fight or flight" approach to conflict. Some of us are conflict linebackers, tackling every issue – and every person connected to every issue – like bulldozers running on nitrous oxide. On the other hand, most of us run from conflict and stay as far away as possible. We allow our hearts to become a junkyard of unresolved hurts that we've inflicted on others and others on us. What we need is a third option: Engage in a biblical process of conflict resolution marked by a spirit of togetherness and a commitment to unity.

Conflict is not fun, but without it we will never establish true community. So go, do life with "those" people, don't be surprised when conflict occurs, and take advantage of the opportunities it affords: opportunities to live out your faith, opportunities to grow, opportunities to show the world how to stay together, how to forgive, how to love.

Worship
Chapter 31 – Colossians 3.16

I hate singing.

Okay, that may be a bit overstated, but the truth isn't far off. I hesitate to tell you this, because someday we might sit together in church, and I've found that after I admit this, people who sit beside me nudge me unless my mouth is moving. Nevertheless, it's true that singing songs about God (or anything else, really) isn't something I wake up hoping I get to do before I go back to sleep.

I'm confessing this, of course, because today we're talking about worship. But before we go any further, we need to clarify something: Worship is more than just singing. Worship literally means ascribing worth to things that are worthy. To worship is to recognize that someone or something is great and then express our appreciation for it. And God is so great that singing alone could hardly express the fullness of his greatness. Matter of fact, worshiping through song can deceive us into thinking that we're good with God when, in fact, we may be the opposite. Worship with our voices must be matched by worship with our lives. Worship encompasses all of life. This is so important that we'll talk more about it tomorrow, but for now we need to talk about singing. Why? Because Paul is setting our agenda, and when Paul begins to describe a life of worship, he speaks about singing.

And be thankful. Let the word of Christ dwell in you richly, teaching and admonishing each other in all wisdom with psalms, hymns, and spiritual songs, singing with gratitude in your hearts to God.

Notice that Paul is describing what happens when the church gathers for worship. This is one of the most detailed descriptions we have of early Christian worship services. As always we're going to break down the details and examine how Paul's words address us today, but first let's dwell on the actual practice of gathering for worship.

"Going to church," as we call it, sometimes gets a bad rap. Just the other day I saw a guy wearing a religious t-shirt. The front simply said, "Don't go to church." (I think we're supposed to think, "Ooh, scandalous.") And on the back a similarly punchy phrase, "Be the church." Now I love the sentiment, because as I just said, God calls us to a life of worship and not just worship services. The problem, though, is that you don't really get one without the other. It's sort of like a basketball shirt saying, "Don't practice" on the front, and "Win basketball games" on the back. Good luck with that. Or more to the point, it's like saying "Don't eat together," but instead "Be a family." Being a family doesn't work very well without eating together. And the church isn't very good at being the church unless we regularly gather for worship.

Paul, for what it's worth, assumes these Jesus-followers will regularly go to church precisely in order to be the church. And assuming they'll gather together, he offers instructions on what to do when they arrive. He provides a grid to structure our time together, and it's a grid most of you will find familiar.

Let's begin with the basic element: singing. Paul mentions three different kinds of songs. We don't want to be too strict about defining the differences, because Paul may simply mean "lots of different kinds of songs." But generally speaking, *psalms* likely refers to worship songs based on the Old Testament book that goes by the same name. *Hymns* are pre-prepared songs that may very include our poem from earlier in Colossians 1.15-20. Some still call them hymns, while others talk about choruses or anthems. And *spiritual songs* may include more spontaneous songs inspired by the Spirit in various situations.

If I could, I'd like to caveat for a minute and speak directly to any men who are reading this. Fellas, I'm just going to be honest (and I hope this doesn't sound sexist): The church is starving for men who will sing. If we sing, the rest of those around us will follow our lead. Trust me, I'm talking to myself as much or more than you. I have no idea how to sing "properly." I don't even know what people mean when they talk about being in the wrong key. I don't like the feeling of thinking other people can hear me. And to be honest, for whatever reason I feel a little silly singing in the first place. But I need to get over myself. And so do you. We need to sing. I have a theory that if more men would sing in worship, our faith would grow, obedience would come more naturally to us, our families would be stronger, and the church would absolutely take off. There's nothing worse than an untested theory, so let's find out if my hunch is correct. Okay, soapbox over. Back to Colossians.

While singing is a basic element of worship, notice how Paul ties it to the church's task of teaching and admonishing one another. This is the second time we've seen this pair of practices, which were set alongside "public proclamation" in 1.28. *Teaching* involves explaining the truth of Scripture in a clear and compelling manner. It is more positive in nature, whereas *admonishing* has the idea of straightening out fuzzy or immature thinking. Admonishing means setting someone's thoughts in proper order by gently correcting misguided beliefs, as well as warning those who might be tempted to walk away or adjust the truth to make it more user-friendly (like the errant teachers in Colossae). In Paul's idea of church, pastors and ministers aren't the only ones who live with the responsibility to communicate truth. Their official efforts must be accompanied by the rest of us engaging one another in conversations over coffee, on our lunch breaks, and in our living rooms – as well as when we "go to church."

Paul defines the content of our singing, as well as our teaching and admonishing: *the word of Christ*. Let the message about Christ *dwell in you richly*, he says. Take everything we've learned about Jesus – about who he is, what he's accomplished, and what he's doing now – and let it *dwell richly*. We're not talking about a superficial or passing dwelling, but a deep and penetrating reality that lingers. May the truth about Jesus take up permanent residence and find a home in our songs and our storytelling and our sermons.

With all this in mind, it isn't hard to understand why, for Paul, corporate worship is flanked on each side by thankfulness. Gratitude expressed in worship is the only sensible response to what God has done for, in, and through us in Christ.

At the end of the day, worship is not about singing. Worship is about God. We aren't singing because we love singing. We are singing because we've caught a glimpse of the greatness of Jesus and therefore have no choice but to express his worth by any means possible. Worship is about what God has done both to create and save us in Christ. And that, even for me, is worth singing about.

Seven
Chapter 32 – Colossians 3.17ff

What if God hates your church's worship services?

It's not a comforting question, nor is it one we typically ask. What could God love more than dozens (or hundreds or thousands) of doting disciples singing and tithing and taking communion and learning the Bible?

But the Bible teaches in multiple places that sometimes God looks at our religious gatherings and wants to vomit. Jesus threatens the church in Laodicea – a very close neighbor to the Colossians – in precisely this fashion in Revelation 3.15-16. This church had a fairly high opinion of themselves, and may indeed have looked fantastic on the outside. But something was wrong. So wrong that Jesus says he will convulsively vomit them out of his mouth. More to our point, God directly attacks some of Israel's worship practices through the Old Testament prophets.

"I hate, I despise your religious festivals; your assemblies are a stench to me. Even though you bring me burnt offerings and grain offerings, I will not accept them. Though you bring choice fellowship offerings, I will have no regard for them. Away with the noise of your songs! I will not listen to the music of your harps." – Amos 5.21-23

"Stop bringing meaningless offerings! Your incense is detestable to me. New Moons, Sabbaths and convocations — I cannot bear your worthless assemblies. Your New Moon feasts and your appointed festivals I hate with all my being. They have become a burden to me; I am weary of bearing them. When you spread out your hands in prayer, I hide my eyes from you; even when you offer many prayers, I am not listening. Your hands are full of blood!"   – Isaiah 1.13-15

Often the specific issue in ancient Israel was their failure to care for the poor. Whoever has ears to hear, let them hear. God does not accept gestures of worship unaccompanied by acts of mercy and justice. More generally, here and elsewhere we see the unbreakable bond between songs that honor God and lives that do the same. Worship is not something you can do for two hours out of every 148. Worship is a seven-days-per-week affair. Worship is a way of life.

Think about how we defined worship yesterday. Worship literally means ascribing worth to things that are worthy. To worship is to recognize that someone or something is great and then express appreciation for it. And today we're going to unpack what we briefly mentioned: God's greatness cannot be adequately expressed except by our entire lives – 24 hours a day, 7 days a week, 52 weeks every year. It isn't by accident that Paul follows up his instructions for gathered worship like this: *And whatever you do, whether in word or deed, do it all in the name of the Lord Jesus, giving thanks to God the Father through him* (Colossians 3.17). All of life has experienced a radical shift in purpose: no longer are our actions, reactions, thoughts, plans, or words aimed at honoring our own name. Nor are they aimed primarily at honoring the name of our industry or company or team or nation or family or church. We live and breathe and move and love *in the name of Jesus*, aiming with our words and deeds to make him famous.

After a statement like that, we expect Paul either to quit while he's ahead or crescendo into some inspirational discourse about taking on the world for Jesus. Instead we get bland instructions regulating our domestic responsibilities. I'm not sure it gets more anti-climactic than Colossians 3.18–4.1.

Remember that Paul is dealing with visionaries who are tempting faithful Jesus-followers to move on from Jesus toward more fulfilling spiritual experiences. And Paul just got through one-upping them by instructing his readers to set their minds and hearts on things above. But here Paul fleshes out the life from above with mundane guidelines about our everyday relationships. This disconnect has led some scholars to suggest that 3.18-4.1 doesn't actually belong to the original letter Paul penned. But surprise at how Paul unfolds his logic reveals our own confusion – we still don't get that spiritual maturity is defined by how we treat one another. By how well we love.

Clearly Paul speaks about relationships within the home, but there are a few things you need to know about the wider context. First of all, ancient households were very different from modern ones. For starters, the home was essentially a business at the same time it was a family. So when we read "household codes" like this one in Colossians, we're seeing "the equivalent of the organizational chart for a modern family business."[43]

Secondly, Paul's overall point – in keeping with the spirit of Colossians 3.17 – seems to be that if Jesus is Lord over anything, he is Lord over everything. More specifically, Jesus is the Lord of our family and work lives every bit as much as our "spiritual" lives. It just so happens that in this section about household relationships, Jesus is referred to as "Lord" exactly seven times. Throughout the ancient world, seven functioned as a number of completeness. Whether or not Paul intentionally drops the hint seven times, the point is clear. Growing up in Christ means not only that we get more Jesus, but that Jesus gets more of us – all of us, to be precise.

What is true of us as the gathered church on Sundays – that we honor Jesus as Lord in word and deed – must be true of us as the scattered church. I remember attending a wonderful little country church in my first few years of college, where one of the elders would always open the worship service with the words, "It's good to be in the house of the Lord this morning." I loved hearing that, because it is good to be gathered in a place designated for focusing on God. But at the same time, it's a dangerous statement. Why is it dangerous? Because it creates the idea that the house of the Lord is a physical place. It's not. The house of the Lord is a people. The house of the Lord is you and me. We don't just go to church. We *are* the church – the spiritual family of folks who know Jesus as our indwelling Lord. And as Paul says here, being the church is every bit as much about Monday through Friday as it is about Sunday.

---

[43] Talbert, 234.

So we are left with a question: Are we allowing Jesus to be Lord of our entire lives? Do our homes reflect our commitment to honor his name in everything?

A pastor was called to serve a small French community, so he began his work by visiting all the homes of those who attended his church. One home he happened to stop by while the wife was away, so he spoke only to the husband. When the man's wife returned, he mentioned the new pastor's visit.

"What did he say?" she asked.

"He asked, 'Does Christ live here?'" the husband replied. "He didn't really ask anything else. Just, 'Does Christ live here?'"

"Well, surely you told him that we're the church's biggest supporters."

"He didn't ask that," the husband said again. "He only asked, 'Does Christ live here?'"

"Okay, but you must have mentioned that we read our Bibles and pray every day."

"You know, he didn't ask about that either. He only asked, 'Does Christ live here?'"

"Well," she persisted, "Did you tell him that we attend services every Sunday and sit in the front row ready to learn and be challenged from God's Word?"

"Honestly, honey, he *didn't ask about anything else.* He only wanted to know, 'Does Christ live here?'"[44]

Let's say someone observed a month of normal life in your home. Would they see the kind of relationships and virtues Paul's describes in Colossians 3.12-17? Do the people living under your roof know that God loves them deeply as his own children? Are your identities securely rooted in him? Are your interactions marked by compassion, gentleness, humility, and patience? Do you approach conflict with a desire to win arguments or a commitment to bearing each other's burdens and mirroring Christ's forgiveness? Do you worship together with the rest of God's people, and is this worship carried over into every area of your lives?

We're going to spend the next few days discussing Paul's specific directives for home and work life, but without these questions as backdrop we're sure to miss the point. There is no part of your world that Jesus

---

[44] Sweet and Viola, 73-74.

doesn't want to rule. Jesus is present every hour of every day, ready to fill each of these moments with his life and lordship. If you aren't worshiping with your life seven days a week, what you do with your lips on Sunday morning doesn't matter one bit. So every time you go home (or anywhere else for that matter), remind yourself, "It's good to be in the house of the Lord." *And whatever you do, whether in word or deed, do it all in the name of the Lord Jesus, giving thanks to God the Father through him.*

Marriage
Chapter 33 – Colossians 3.18-19

It has been said that if love is one long sweet dream, marriage is the alarm clock. Or that if love is blind, marriage is an eye-opener. Or that man is incomplete until he gets married, at which point he is totally finished. Search "marriage jokes" on the Internet and you'll find these and other (mostly pessimistic) clichés about wedded non-bliss. Whether marriage is an easy target I can't say for sure, but it's definitely a common one.

I've long felt that marriage is one of God's most brilliant and most ridiculous ideas. Brilliant because no relationship provides greater opportunity for growth in love or healing of past wounds. Ridiculous because it trusts actual human beings with such delicate and generation-altering realities. Nevertheless, marriage stands near the center of God's purposes for the world and at the top of Paul's household instructions.

Attending to the immediate context will set the stage for Paul's principles on marriage. Notice first that this follows Paul's general command to do everything in the name of Jesus. Here Paul makes explicit what we might have assumed: *Whatever you do* includes the way we treat our spouses. Also keep in mind that Paul isn't just issuing commands we're called to follow by our strength. Paul laid a foundation for these exhortations grounded in the fact that God is currently working to transform us. He has injected into our spiritual bloodstream the DNA of God's perfect kingdom, and according to this new wiring we are being renewed daily so that we look increasingly more like what he initially intended. We are being restored to our original destiny.

Speaking of our original destiny raises what might be the most important question regarding marriage: What is marriage for? What is its purpose? Confusion on this question lies behind much of the marital crisis our culture is currently experiencing. We've all heard the divorce rate statistics, not that you needed numbers to confirm what most of us have lived through in some capacity.

Sociologist Anthony Giddens explains that marriage in our world has become what's called a "pure relationship."[45] He doesn't mean "pure" in a sexual sense, but rather in the sense of marriage's purpose. In the past, marriage served all sorts of functions. In pre-industrial societies, marriage relationships were by definition business partnerships as well. Husbands needed wives and wives needed husbands simply to make ends meet. Bearing children factored into this equation as well. The children served the family, and the marriage provided a psychologically safe environment for kids to grow up and contribute. But as society developed and independence became more of a reality, marriage lost its missional basis. Marriage turned inward. Now, generally speaking, the purpose of marriage has been reduced to making each other happy. This is what "pure relationship" means. No external driving forces keep husbands and wives together. Marriage has become a relationship that exists purely for itself.

Making your husband or wife happy certainly isn't bad, but that's a lot of pressure! But marriages created for the purpose of mutual happiness are difficult to sustain during the inevitable dry spells or hard times. What's more, this view of marriage hardly takes into account the teachings of Scripture.

Taking our cues from the context of Colossians 3.18-19, let's think through the question of what marriage is for. First, we must again mention that the purpose of marriage is to honor the name of Jesus. Colossians 3.17 couldn't make this point any clearer. Husbands, how you treat your wife should make people think of Jesus. Wives, how you treat your husbands should bring honor to his name.

Second, marriage provides endless opportunities to grow by reflecting God's love to others. Since spiritual maturity is measured not by Bible

---

[45] Anthony Giddens, *Modernity and Self-Identity* (Stanford University Press, 1991), 10-14.

knowledge or church attendance but how we treat one another, marriage becomes the first place for married Jesus-followers to take our faith to the next level. We've been talking this week about how God's work in our lives is always communal. We are being built together as the church. And whether during conflict or while gathered in worship, we are learning how to actually be the church. We are learning how to love. Marriage is community at its hardest and finest. Marriage, like the church as a whole, is a school of love.

Third, looking ahead to next week, marriage forms the backbone of homes committed to extending God's mission in the world. It isn't by accident that the husband-wife relationship comes first in Paul's household code. Get this wrong and the rest will reflect something less than God's ideal. Get this right and our homes as well as our workplaces will become vehicles God works through to advance his reign of love. The purpose of marriage is to show the world what God's love looks like in action.

With these brief but important thoughts in mind, let's look at what Paul says: *Wives, place yourselves under your husbands, as is fitting in the Lord. Husbands, love your wives and do not resent them* (Colossians 3.18-19).

At this point about half of you are saying, "Hey, why did you soften the text? The actual word is 'submit'!" And the other half is bristling at the suggestion that women – or anyone else, for that matter – should *place themselves under* anyone. Some people think these instructions have nothing to do with Paul's culture and that they provide God's unbendable model for how homes should operate. Others want to redefine familial roles based on how our culture has shifted away from Paul's. I'm certainly not naïve enough to think I can solve this debate in one short chapter, nor do I think either side is without problems.

We must indeed read Paul's words in light of his own world. While telling women to submit seems scandalous to us, commanding husbands to limit their power through love had a similar impact back then. It's not that husbands never loved their wives. They did. But in codes like this you'd expect husbands to be told to keep their wives in check, or something similar. By contrast, in Ephesians Paul sets these same commands within the practice of *mutual* submission (Ephesians 5.21-22).

Here in Colossians, Paul similarly pushes the envelope toward something like what we'd call equality. And at the very least, we must admit that "the model of the wife staying home to engage mainly in childrearing while the husband participates in the work force is an ideal of the relatively leisured, nineteenth-century U.S. middle class, and was not common through most of Western history," much less biblical history.[46] Paul simply isn't talking about who should make more money, pick the kids up from school, or clean the dishes.

Having said that, it would take a bold – and arguably naïve – person to suggest that marriage in our world has vastly improved upon models from the ancient church. Rejecting Paul's wisdom won't exactly set you up for marital success.

I know I've taken a while to get to the point, but in the end what Paul says isn't overly complex: Marriage works best when husbands sacrificially serve their wives and wives gently respect their husbands. Paul addresses both husbands and wives as mature adults who must take responsibility for their own contribution to healthy homes. Husbands are not told to demand deference or put wives in their place; the exhortation is to the wife alone. Likewise, husbands are to take responsibility to love their wives and not "to become bitter or angry when she turns out to be, like him, a real human being, and not merely the projection of his own hopes or fantasies."[47]

Emerson Eggerichs has fleshed out this concept in his highly practical book *Love and Respect*. He sees in Paul's words a cycle that manifests itself for better or worse in all marriages. They asked this question to 7,000 people: "When you are in a conflict with your spouse or significant other, do you feel unloved or disrespected?" Over 70% of the women said "unloved" and over 80% of the men said "disrespected."[48] Apparently Paul knows something about how marriage works in every era. Of course this doesn't mean men don't need love and women don't need respect. Both matter to all of us. But marital breakdown typically begins when husbands fail to love their wives or when wives disrespect their husbands. This sets in motion a destructive back-and-forth cycle that squeezes the life out of even "Christian" homes.

Husbands, if you don't feel you're getting respect, ask yourself if you're giving love. Wives, if you don't feel loved, ask whether your husband feels

---

[46] Craig Keener, *Paul, Women, & Wives* (Peabody: Hendrickon, 1992), 227. He adds, "A man who wants to imitate Jesus cannot be some epitome of macho masculinity with a beer in one hand and a television control in the other, snapping out orders while his wife is at his beck and call."

[47] Wright, 151.

[48] Emerson Eggerichs, *Love and Respect* (Nashville: Thomas Nelson, 2004).

respected. Then both of you right the ship by following Paul's instructions. Lean on God's love for you and give to your spouse the love and/or respect they need.

If your marriage is hurting, get help today. Marriage is too important – and life is too short – to passively allow your home to descend further away from God's design. Do whatever it takes to make things right, and watch God not only increase your own joy but also work through your Christ-centered family to bring life and healing to others.

Parenting
Chapter 34 – Colossians 3.20-21

My daughter has always served as an endless source of adorableness. When she was younger we were working on animal sounds around the same time we taught her that her little toes go to the marketplace, eat roast beef, and so on. Frequently we would have the following conversation:

"Claire, what sound does a cow make?"

"Mooooooo."

"What sounds does a dog make?"

"Woof, woof."

"What sound does a cat make?"

"Meow."

"What sound does a sheep make?"

"Baa, baa."

"What sound does a monkey make?"

"Ooh, ooh, aah, aah."

"What sound does a piggy make?"

"Wee, wee, wee."

I went into a brief depression when she realized the correct answer was "Oink, oink," because "Wee, wee, wee" was the most precious thing I'd ever heard.

Some time ago I was away from my family for a couple weeks. When I left Claire could say her ABCs up to D. When I got back she could sing the entire song. Only one problem. You know how after Z you do that little closing bit? "Now I know my A-B-Cs, next time won't you sing with me?" Well she hadn't quite figured that part out. Instead she sang, "Now I know my A-B-C-D-E-F-G-..." It was a little sad, but a lot adorable.

Kids are cute. If being mommies and daddies involved nothing more than enjoying and celebrating their cuteness, then parenting would be easy.

But parenting isn't easy. Parenting isn't easy because some cute little kids grow up to be bratty teenagers or, even worse, horrifyingly evil adults. We know this (even if we don't often put it so starkly), so we try to do our best to avoid complete disaster. But we don't always know if by doing our best we're doing what actually is best. Parenting isn't easy because we know how much is riding on the line, and yet we don't have an official daily scorecard to evaluate our performance or measure our progress.

Maybe this is why parenting styles can be such a lightning rod conversation topic. If you don't believe me, walk into a room of new parents (particularly new moms) and say, "What do you think about Babywise?" Or, "Should we spank our kids?" Then sit back and watch. Soon you'll understand why parenting styles should be added to politics and religion as subjects you only bring up when you want to start a fight.

Specific strategies aside, the wisest parents I know emphasize the fact that we're not just raising kids. We're raising adults. We're not trying to produce the best possible 6 or 16-year-olds, but rather the sanest and wisest possible 25, 35, and 45-year-olds. Raising good adults is complicated, unpredictable, and scary. Raising good adults is difficult.

Thankfully, we're not alone. We have each other, the wisdom of past generations, and more books than we could ever read. Above all this, we have the Bible. The Bible is hardly a detailed parenting manual, and if we hope to find in its pages guidance for every possible parental conundrum, we will be disappointed. (And we might get put in jail. Whatever you do, don't follow Jephthah's example![49]) The Bible does, however, provide basic principles that form the foundation for faithful parenting. Few places crystallize this wisdom as succinctly as Colossians 3.19-20: *Children, obey your parents in all things, for this is pleasing in the Lord. Fathers, don't push your children too hard, so they don't become discouraged.*

---

[49] Jephthah once vowed to sacrifice whatever came through his door, which backfired when his daughter walked out to meet him (Judges 11.29-40). Thankfully, one larger point of the book of Judges is that God moves his mission forward *in spite of* rebellious people and inept leaders.

Notice first that Paul addresses fathers specifically, rather than fathers and mothers. Is Paul saying that the parenting task falls squarely on the shoulders of dads? Of course not. He mentions fathers because in Paul's world fathers were the sole unquestioned authority in all family affairs (at least in theory). What he says applies to both fathers and mothers.

Having said this, however, we'd be foolish to underemphasize the importance of dads for the health of our families. A few years back, results were released of a massive study on church attendance and passing on the faith from generation to generation. Their primary finding was that above all other factors, the religious practices of the father determine whether children will attend church when they move out on their own. If the father does not come to church at all but the mother does, 2% of children will become regular adult worshippers. If the father comes some of the time and mother comes regularly, 3% will join the faithful. But if both father and mother attend regularly, 33% of their children will end up as regular churchgoers. That's over ten times more! And another 41% will attend at least some of the time. Dads, if we do not go to church, no matter how faithful our wives may be, only 2% of our kids will go on to worship regularly. If we do, over 70% of our kids will likely participate in church as adults, and half of that number will be more than just casual attenders.

Church attendance is just the tip of the iceberg. For instance, over 70% of pregnant teenagers grew up with absent or disengaged dads. Almost 85% of young men in prison come from homes without a father. Sixty-five percent of suicide victims live in fatherless homes, as do over 70% of drug users. [50]

These sobering statistics ought to wake up all dads everywhere. Fatherlessness – the kind where dads are literally gone as well as the kind where dads might as well be – is one of the crippling social ills of our time. Men, our families are dying because we are too selfish to stay with them or too busy to pay them mind. I'm not trying to preach at you. I get it. For whatever reasons, it's sometimes just easier to disengage. We're busy. We already feel like we're doing our best and we fear it's not good enough. We may be great with numbers or machines or customers, but we don't know

---

[50] See John Sowers, *Fatherless Generation* (Grand Rapids: Zondervan, 2010). For the church attendance stats, see Richard Egan, "Church Attendance: The Family, Feminism, and the Declining Role of Fatherhood." http://www.ad2000.com.au/articles/2002/sep2002p8_1115.html. Accessed 7/1/12.

what to say to our teenagers. We have little idea how to improve, and we fear incompetence more than death. But we must face the facts, and the fact is that we have a simple choice: Engage our families and lead them spiritually, or watch our kids drift further and further away from the God who sent his only Son to bring them home.

Dads (and moms), if you have walked out on your family, do whatever it takes to make things right. Don't expect your re-entry – whether literally moving back into your homes or simply moving back into your kids' lives – to be easy or smooth. They may harbor bitterness toward you, as you may toward them. But we have no other option. And if you live at home, do whatever is necessary to "bring up your children in the training and instruction of the Lord," as Paul put it in Ephesians 6.4. The greatest thing you can do for your kids is to train them to trust and follow Jesus.

How? So glad you asked.

Simply put, Paul sees two principles at work in faithful parenting.[51] The first is gentleness. *Don't push your children too hard, so they don't become discouraged.* Paul's world held to an idea known as *patria potestas*, which essentially meant the Father had virtually unlimited power over his children. Here Paul speaks not of the power at their disposal, but the importance of corralling it. We shouldn't hound our kids so much that they give up trying to please us. If they become dispirited to the point of quitting, we have a problem. Likewise if they mask their discouragement with false arrogance or anxious self-assertion. We must build our kids' sense of value, not tear it down.

Having said that, notice that this command works within the assumption that parents set the agenda for their kids. We provide clear boundaries and engage in serious and appropriate discipline. Letting kids run the home has become just as much a problem in our world as being too strict. Paul's command for children to obey their parents establishes the other half of his basic philosophy of successful parenting: mothers and fathers are the authority in the home. We are the law. Children's basic stance is one of obedience. By extension, parents' basic responsibility is to tell our kids what to do. Earlier I quoted Paul's words from the same teaching in Ephesians that provide the grid for what we tell them to do: we

---

[51] Paul addresses both parents and children, but for space purposes we're focusing on the responsibility of the parents. Children, you should be able to pick up from this discussion how to play your part in building healthy families.

bring them up in the training and instruction of the Lord. We don't fall into the "I'm going to let my kids find their own course in life" trap. Trusting children to "find their own way" in this world or "discover what to believe on their own" – without the proper training in Christ-centered discernment – is about as wise and loving as dropping someone in the ocean before teaching them how to swim.

We love our kids by authoritatively teaching them how to live well in Christ, always being mindful of the danger of pushing too hard. Simple? Sure it is. But not necessarily easy. Then again, who said raising adults should be easy?

Work
Chapter 35 – Colossians 3.22–4.1

Work was not our idea. Work was part of God's original design for creation. God's first command to men and women was to make babies and then get to work. We were given the task of extending God's dominion throughout the world. We were instructed to cultivate creation's fruitfulness through organization and planning and division of labor and good old-fashioned blood, sweat, and tears. We were made to work. This means, by definition, that work is good. We must be clear on this point before we move any further. Work is not part of the curse we brought on ourselves through sin. Work is good.

Having said that, work, like everything else, has been affected by our fall from original goodness. Work, though good, bears the marks of sin's curse in many ways. If you informally surveyed ten people and asked, "What is frustrating about your job?" or "What is wrong with your workplace or industry?" you would get twenty different answers, at least half of them completely legitimate.

Today we're going to talk about work in a wounded world. From this starting point we could go any number of ways: the fact that those who work the hardest don't make the most money, or that some bad people inherit great jobs while many good people stand in the unemployment line, or that some entire industries play by rules explicitly designed to destroy the environment or human dignity or the glory of God.

But in sticking with our plan, we'll take our cues from the apostle Paul. Here in Colossians 3.22–4.1 he speaks about the strain between what we often call management and labor.

Slaves, in all things obey your earthly masters, not just when they're looking – as if you were just pleasing men – but with a sincere heart, fearing the Lord. Whatever you do, work from the soul, as if for the Lord and not for a human, knowing that from the Lord you will receive the rewarded inheritance. Serve this Lord – Christ – for anyone acting unjustly will receive back injustice for his actions, and there is no partiality. Masters, provide justice and fairness for the slaves, knowing that you also have a Master in heaven.

Maybe you've heard about the man in a hot air balloon who realized he was lost. He reduced altitude and spotted a woman below. He descended a bit more and shouted, "Excuse me, can you help me? I promised a friend I would meet him an hour ago, but I don't know where I am."

The woman replied, "You're in a hot air balloon hovering approximately 30 feet above the ground. You're between 40 and 41 degrees north latitude and between 59 and 60 degrees west longitude."

"You must be an engineer," said the balloonist.

"I am," replied the woman, "How did you know?"

"Well," answered the balloonist, "everything you told me is technically correct, but I have no idea what to make of your information, and the fact is I'm still lost. Frankly, you've not been much help at all. If anything, you've delayed my trip."

The woman below responded, "You must be in management."

"I am," replied the balloonist, "but how did you know?"

"Well," said the woman, "you don't know where you are or where you're going. You have risen to where you are due to a large quantity of hot air. You made a promise, which you've no idea how to keep, and you expect people beneath you to solve your problems. The fact is you are in exactly the same position you were in before we met, but now, somehow, it's my fault."[52]

---

[52] http://tiny.cc/management-labor. Accessed 7/15/12.

Tension is no stranger to the relationship between employers and employees. But before we discuss this tension further in light of what Paul says, we need to address the elephant in this text. To put it simply, this passage isn't about "work" per se. It's about slavery. This raises two questions we need to briefly address: Why interpret a text about slavery as a text about work? Why didn't Paul push for complete abolition of slavery? The first is simple: what Paul says to masters and slaves isn't that hard to translate into the categories of employers and employees. In both cases one person or group has power over another, and this imbalance of power often produces particular kinds of conflict.

The second question is a bit more complicated. As twenty-first century Jesus-followers, we find Paul's apparent acceptance of slavery a little confusing, and, perhaps, embarrassing. Why trust Paul if he okays such a horrific institution? Let me offer four quick points in response.

First, we need to remember that "slavery" has more than one meaning, and what comes to mind for many Americans is different from the slavery Paul knew. Slaves in the ancient world were trusted with different kinds of tasks depending on ability and training, some of which were not at all backbreaking or degrading. However, slaves were still considered property, so we shouldn't pretend slavery was generally desirable.

Second, we need to read what Paul says here in light of the overall arc of Scripture on this issue. In Philemon, another letter Paul wrote to the churches in Colossae, Paul goes a few steps further in undermining the institution of slavery – gently demanding that a slave owner accept his ex-runaway slave as an equal. Generally speaking, the Bible moves progressively further and further away from uncritical acceptance of slavery, so we should follow that trajectory to its logical conclusion.

Third, Paul doesn't protest against the institution of slavery because that would be about as useful as us protesting against the Internet. Nothing we can say or do is going to rid the world of the Internet, at least not in the near future. Our only option is to figure out how best to navigate our way through the digital age. No doubt Paul's knowledge of recent history taught him that attempts to destroy slavery had proved futile in revolts of 134-131, 103-100, and 73-71 BC. At least in this letter, Paul the pastor opts for the more modest goal of helping his people make the best of a less-than-ideal situation.

Fourth, what Paul says here is more radical than we might think. Simply the fact that Paul addresses slaves is noteworthy. By speaking directly to them he affirms their value as substantial members of the community. Also notice that five times Paul mentions Jesus as *Lord*. Both slave and master answer to their common Master Jesus, which puts them on equal footing in the relationship that matters most. And Paul's actual instructions push far beyond what was normal in his world. A slave owner was obligated by law only to feed and clothe his slaves. Paul clearly goes way beyond this. Talk of justice and fairness would have struck most slave-owners as extraordinary and even outrageous. Paul essentially undermines slavery by questioning its accepted rules and assumptions, sowing seeds that are still in process of coming to full bloom.

With all this in mind, let's get back to work. Paul offers five basic principles in this text. To employees, he says the following:

(1) *Do your job.* "Obedience" may not always be an appropriate word to describe an employee's response to an employer's requests, but the principle remains: Do what you signed up to do. Obviously this doesn't apply if you're told to do anything that dishonors Christ. And you always have the option of resigning. But generally speaking, your job is to do your job.

(2) *Work hard all the time.* Literally Paul says to *work from the soul*, which means wholeheartedly or without reservation. Laziness is not a virtue, whether the type that sits on the couch or the kind that gravitates to the water cooler (or social network websites). If you are not working hard, God is displeased with this part of your life.

(3) *Remember who you work for.* Paul emphasizes the still common problem of people working hard only when under the supervisor's eye. Looking like you're working hard is not the same thing as working hard. Paul's problem with faking it is that our real boss is always watching. Three times Paul repeats *Serve the Lord*, indicating the importance of knowing who we work for. We work for Jesus. We aim to please him. Remember this when you finish your lunch break or head to the office in the morning. Your ultimate Lord is not the Customer Service Manager, the CEO, the Board of Trustees, or the stock market. Your one and only Lord is Jesus. Serve him.

And to management he gives these two principles:

(1) *Don't abuse your power.* You are in a position of power over others. You can (a) use your power to enhance your own position, prestige, or bank account; or (b) use it to serve those above you (which is often another way of accomplishing (a)); or (c) use it to serve those "under" you. Paul, like Jesus, favors the latter. You are in a position of leadership for the sake of those you're leading, not the other way around. Your responsibility, as Paul names it here, is to provide justice and fairness for everyone.

(2) *Remember who you work for.* No matter who you are, no matter how much power you have, you don't sit atop the totem pole. If you are 100 yards above your employees, Jesus is miles higher than you. You are, in the final analysis, very small.

God's answer to the problem of work in a broken world is the church – a community of both managers and laborers who together submit to Jesus, and from this center go on to perform their respective roles with diligence and grace. Work has fallen far from God's original intent. But by following Paul's guidance – in other words, by remembering Jesus our Lord – we'll move closer toward the dream God envisioned when he invented it.

moreJESUS part 6 – MISSION

In *A Million Miles in a Thousand Years*, Donald Miller tells about how his friend Jason saved his family. Over lunch one day Jason was venting about his thirteen-year-old daughter who was dating a loser, had just been caught smoking marijuana, and couldn't care less what mom or dad said. Miller fired back his diagnosis: she was living a terrible story.

Neither had any idea what he meant, but the more they talked it out the more they realized they were stumbling onto something profound. All good stories are driven by characters who want something worthwhile and overcome hardship to get it.

That night Jason couldn't sleep. He realized that he hadn't provided his daughter with a significant part in an interesting story. So she found another story, another adventure – one she mattered in, even if "mattering" meant being used.

Determined to deliver his family a better story, he found an organization that builds orphanages around the world for $25,000 a piece. With no idea how they'd raise the money – and before even talking to his wife – he signed them up, called a family meeting, and revealed his grand plan. They were, um, not happy – his daughter because he was ruining her life, and his wife because he was ruining their daughter's life without letting her in on the fun.

To make a long story short, his wife was in the end very proud of him, and his daughter came around too. She ditched the dude, tossed the pot, and started talking to her parents again. As Jason later put it, "No girl who plays the role of a hero dates a guy who uses her."[53]

Some of us live miserable – or at best boring – lives because we inhabit crappy stories. We lack a purpose that's worth our time. We've been sent on the wrong mission.

I'm typing these words from Antioch, the birthplace of Christian missions. "Missions" refers to the intentional spreading of the gospel from one culture to another. While the mission is much broader than missions in this sense, cross-cultural gospel work nevertheless discloses something essential to the mission: the realization that you and I are not the only ones

---

[53] Donald Miller, *A Million Miles in a Thousand Years* (Nashville: Thomas Nelson, 2011), 49-54.

who need more Jesus. The entire world needs more Jesus. What's more, Jesus deserves the entire world's faithful obedience.

So we've been sent. So we go. So we live. On mission.

In one sense, our mission is rooted in the final earthly words of Jesus:

"All authority in heaven and on earth has been given to me. Therefore go and make disciples of all nations, baptizing them in the name of the Father and of the Son and of the Holy Spirit, and teaching them to obey everything I have commanded you. And surely I am with you always, to the very end of the age."   – Matthew 28.18-20

"The Messiah will suffer and rise from the dead on the third day, and repentance for the forgiveness of sins will be preached in his name to all nations, beginning at Jerusalem . . . You will receive power when the Holy Spirit comes on you; and you will be my witnesses in Jerusalem, and in all Judea and Samaria, and to the ends of the earth."
– Luke 24.47; Acts 1.8

Jesus said, "Peace be with you! As the Father has sent me, I am sending you."   – John 20.21

But more broadly, Jesus' words catapult us into the final chapters of a story begun long before he spoke them. By now you know we're talking about the fulfillment of God's original promise to Abraham, later crystallized as his dream for ancient Israel. To the former God announced in Genesis 12.2-3:

I will make you into a great nation, and I will bless you; I will make your name great, and you will be a blessing. I will bless those who bless you, and whoever curses you I will curse; and all peoples on earth will be blessed through you.

And to the latter in Isaiah 42.6-7:

I, the LORD, have called you in righteousness; I will take hold of your hand. I will keep you and will make you to be a covenant for the people and a light for the Gentiles, to open eyes that are blind, to free captives from prison and to release from the dungeon those who sit in darkness.

Jesus fulfilled these promises and bequeathed the continuation of God's mission to the church. He wrote us into The Story. But living on mission turned out to be more complicated than the first Jesus-followers anticipated. When God said he planned to bless all families through this one, when he told Israel they were to become a light to all nations, when he announced that he wasn't afraid to call hated enemies like Egypt and Assyria his adopted children alongside Israel, they didn't think he was really serious. At least they didn't expect it to play out like this. Sure the Gentiles can benefit from our Messiah, they reasoned, but they've certainly got to become Jews first!

Apparently not.

I forgot to tell you what happened here in Antioch. To make a long story short, the earliest Jesus-followers were Jews who, after coming to faith in Jesus as Messiah, spread this message to other Jews. But soon funny things started happening:

> Now those who had been scattered by the persecution that broke out when Stephen was killed traveled as far as Phoenicia, Cyprus and Antioch, spreading the word only among Jews. Some of them, however, men from Cyprus and Cyrene, went to Antioch and began to speak to Greeks also, telling the good news about the Lord Jesus. The Lord's hand was with them, and a great number of people believed and turned to the Lord.   – Acts 11.19-21

The church learned a lesson here that we must never forget: The good news of Jesus isn't just for us. The gospel is also for people who don't look like us, eat like us, or talk like us. The gospel is for everyone.

So we've been sent. So we go. So we live. On mission.

Prayer
Chapter 36 – Colossians 4.2-6

Mission begins in prayer because mission begins with God. Living on mission wasn't some genius or sage or apostle's great idea. Living missionally is the only sane response to a God who is on the move. And because mission begins and ends with the movement of God, mission begins in prayer.

> *Continue persistently in prayer, staying alert in it with thanksgiving, and also praying for us so that God might open to us a door for the word, so we can tell the mystery of Christ for which I have been bound, so that I might disclose it appropriately.* — Colossians 4.2-6

The original Greek sentence literally begins with the word prayer. "Prayer – continue in it!" Grammatically, theologically, and missionally, prayer comes first.

It might help to know you're not the first person – or the first church – to find prayer challenging. The opening verb means "adhere to" or "persist in" and may suggest a desire to give up. When we pray we acknowledge our dependence on someone greater than ourselves, which isn't easy for us. Perhaps our problems in prayer stem from our discomfort with depending on what we cannot control, and we can hardly control someone we cannot see.

Yet we pray, and when we pray we acknowledge God as the initiator of and authority over the mission we are attempting to advance.

Sometimes as a child my friends or mentors would teach me things that I had already learned from my mom. I would come home announcing some great new insight I never would've received were it not for this wonderfully wise person in my life. She was rightly annoyed over my apparent inability to learn the same truth from her. Authority doesn't typically like competition.

In prayer we give God our requests as well as our ear, and in this way we unapologetically risk offending all other sources of authority and blessing. Prayer is an act of defiance.

Prayer is an act of personal defiance, because in prayer we minimize ourselves. Prayer doesn't come easy for people who value liberty and autonomy above all. Self-reliance is the only reliance our world celebrates, but in prayer we take our cues from someone other than the mirror. Mission doesn't begin with planning or studying or preaching or fundraising or talking to neighbors. We don't start with our knowledge or gifts or cleverness. In prayer we put ourselves in our place, which is second at best. In prayer we submit both our adequacies and inadequacies to Christ who is all in all.

Prayer is an act of spiritual defiance, because in prayer we disregard any spiritual being or influence or idea that is below Christ – which is to say, all of them. Like the Colossians we are tempted to spread our spiritual reliance among many potential helpers – a dash of angel here, a pinch of astrology there, some self-help over in the corner. Knowing our tendencies in this regard, we pray to this God and no other.

Prayer is an act of political defiance, because in prayer we marginalize the powers that be. So often we think we could solve the world's problems if we could just get our hands on policy. Whether your beef is eliminating poverty or penitential racism on the one hand, or getting prayer in schools and defending biblical marriage on the other, Jesus-followers on the Right and Left often over-trust political power. To fight this tendency, we pray.

We pray because while we respect all legitimate earthly authorities, we know an Authority and Power compared to whom "the nations are like a drop in a bucket; they are regarded as dust on the scales; he weighs the islands as though they were fine dust" (Isaiah 40.15). And again, "Before him all the nations are as nothing; they are regarded by him as worthless and less than nothing" (40.17). No wonder the prophet then asks, "With whom, then, will you compare God?" And since with the prophets we answer, "No one," we begin with prayer.

Finally, prayer is even an act of ecclesial defiance. "Ecclesial" simply means having to do with the church. We spent all last week emphasizing the community of faith's importance for the growth of God's kingdom. But in prayer, even our dependence upon one another is demoted in favor of our reliance on God. We need each other, but we need God more and first.

Prayer is an act of defiance because prayer leaves God alone at the top where he belongs.

Thankfully, Paul doesn't just talk about the theory or importance of prayer. Here in Colossians 4.2-6, he provides four guidelines for our actual praying:

(1) Pray consistently rather than haphazardly. Right out of the gate Paul reminds us to make prayer a steady fixture in our regular routine. Notice how different Bible versions translate the opening words: Devote yourself to prayer. Continue steadfastly in prayer. Keep on praying. Keep persisting in prayer. Persevere in prayer. Continue earnestly in prayer. Spend a lot of time in prayer. Pray diligently.

Clearly we don't just pray on occasion or only when we feel a specific need. Instead we "make prayer a standard feature" of our lives.[54]

So when is the last time you prayed? Or more strategically, where do you have prayer written into your schedule? Fewer authorities in our culture are as thoroughly respected as appointment calendars, so write prayer in. If when someone invites you out, you say, "I can't come because I'll be praying," first they'll look at you like a pretentious twit, and if they still want you to come they'll say, "You can pray anytime. Come with us." But if you say, "I have a previously scheduled meeting in my calendar," they won't think twice about it.[55]

Haphazard prayer eventually becomes non-existent prayer. So be devoted to prayer.

(2) Pray alertly rather than lazily. Some people think that by mentioning alertness, Paul warns us to be mindful of Jesus' return. We pray with the anticipation that at some point our prayer will turn into actual conversation

---

[54] Moo, 319.

[55] Eugene Peterson, *The Contemplative Pastor* (Grand Rapids: Eerdmans, 1989), 22-23.

and our world will find the healing we desperately seek. This is possible, but more likely Paul issues a general warning against complacency and absent-mindedness. There is a time to daydream in God's presence, and no doubt he enjoys this just as much as when our own children climb onto our laps for no particular purpose. But during specific times of prayer we ought to focus and stay mindful of our tendency to mentally meander. In light of the situation in Colossae, Paul also probably wants his readers to stay alert so that wrong ideas about God and Jesus don't contaminate our prayers. Finally, as we exit the proverbial prayer closet, we carry with us an alert attentiveness to God's presence all around.

(3) Pray gratefully rather than anxiously. Prayer is the place to pour out even the ugly parts of our heart to God. God knows and cares about every detail of your life. And most prayers in the Bible include people asking God for what they think they need. But prayer must never be reduced to a therapy session for complaining or, even worse, demanding. Prayer begins with God and God has been ridiculously good to us, so prayer ought to be marked by thanksgiving. This is the sixth and final time Paul mentions being thankful in Colossians. Thanksgiving always accompanies a proper knowledge of all God has accomplished in Christ. Gratitude for God's good gifts – both spiritual and material – protects us against false teaching and misguided praying. Prayer begins and ends with thankfulness.

(4) Pray missionally rather than selfishly. Once again I want to be clear that God cares about everything going on in your life and in our world. But prayers for our pets or even for the sick should not occupy the majority of our time talking to God. Paul's suggested prayer is not for personal benefit but the growth of the gospel. He doesn't even pray for an open door for himself, but only for the Word or message about Christ. All he asks for himself is that he wouldn't get in its way.

And so we end where we began. With prayer, and therefore with mission. With mission, and therefore with prayer. Take away prayer and mission becomes nothing but one more human program for personal or social transformation. It won't work. Take away mission and prayer gets transformed from a "wartime walkie-talkie" into "domestic intercom for increasing our conveniences."[56] We pray as we live on mission. We've been sent on mission and therefore we pray.

---

[56] John Piper, *Desiring God* (Colorado Springs: Multnomah, 2003), 178.

Action

Chapter 37 – Colossians 4.5-6

Something about the early Christians caught the world's attention.

If, as many scholars suggest, by the time of Constantine (in the early 300s) around 10% of the population had become Christians, then the church grew by an average of 40% per decade during the first three hundred years after the time of Jesus.

Impressive numbers under any circumstances, these growth rates borderline on ridiculous when you consider the various waves of persecution – some local and informal, some state-sponsored and empire-wide – that inflicted the church over its first two-and-a-half centuries. Contemplate, for instance, the fact that even during times of peace, lots of people flat out hated the Jesus movement. Consider the following quote:

> [Christians are] a gang . . . of discredited and proscribed desperadoes who band themselves against the gods. Fellows who gather together illiterates from the dregs of the populace and credulous women with the instability natural to their sex, and so organize a rabble of profane conspirators, leagued together by meetings at night and ritual fasts and unnatural repasts . . . a secret tribe that shuns the light, silent in the open, but talkative in hid corners . . . Root and branch it must be exterminated and accursed.
>
> – Minicius Felix, *Octavius* 8.4, 9.1-2

From very early on Jesus-followers were considered atheistic (for not believing in Roman gods and goddesses), anti-social, unpatriotic, and a threat to the stability of the empire.

Yet people persisted in converting to Christianity in ever-increasing numbers. Why?

It wasn't for reasons we might think. Church folks weren't canvassing the marketplace handing out gospel tracts or asking people where they'd go if they died that very night. Even haters observed that to some degree they were "silent in the open," as the quote above attests. This doesn't mean Jesus-followers didn't talk about their faith – quite the opposite, as we'll soon see – but they were careful about it to say the least. (You probably would be too if it meant keeping your life and protecting your friends!)

At any rate, they didn't have big "evangelism" programs or events. Neither did they have outwardly attractive worship services.[57]

Something about the early Christians caught the world's attention, and it wasn't what they said. It was what they did. It was how they lived.

Fourth-century Roman Emperor Julian (AD 331-363) found the church's growth disgusting, and thus devoted quite a bit of energy to halting the "sickening" advance of Christianity. He saw quite clearly the role good deeds played in foiling his dream. He wrote the following to one of his pagan priests:

> We must pay special attention to this point, and by this means effect a cure. For when it came about that the poor were neglected and overlooked by the [pagan] priests, then I think the impious Galileans [Christians] observed this fact and devoted themselves to philanthropy. And they have gained ascendancy in the words of their deeds through the credit they win for such practices . . . They begin with their so-called love-feast, or hospitality, or service of tables . . . and the result is that they have led very many into atheism [i.e. Christianity].[58]

---

[57] This probably goes without saying, but I am certainly not discrediting such evangelism efforts, nor am I knocking inviting worship settings. In another place, Paul specifically says to evaluate your worship services in part based on whether or not guests will think you're crazy (see 1 Corinthians 14). I'm just observing that these weren't the ways the early churches operated and therefore couldn't have been the reasons for such phenomenal growth.

[58] Emperor Julian, "Fragment of a Letter to a Priest," in *The Works of the Emperor Julian* (Loeb Classical Library 157), 3:67-73.

Octavius observed in friendlier terms, *"Beauty of life encourages strangers to join the ranks . . . We do not preach great things, but we live them."*[59] The way they lived their lives was, in the words of one historian, "rumor worthy" and "question posing."[60] People noticed. And when people notice, eventually they ask.

Walk wisely toward outsiders, capitalizing on the moment. May your speech always be gracious, seasoned with salt so you'll know how you should answer each person.   – Colossians 4.5-6

You can't answer people who aren't asking questions. Paul worked with the assumption that our unique way of life will move others to ask questions about why we do what we do. We *walk wisely.* We follow the pattern we see in Christ, who happens to be the template for authentic humanity. We treat others well, whether or not they belong to our little club. We walk unburdened by joy-thieves such as past mistakes, present imperfections, or future uncertainties. Something deep within people's souls resonates with how we love and hope and believe.

This should hardly surprise us. Peter clearly assumes the same possibility: "Live such good lives among the pagans that, though they accuse you of doing wrong, they may see your good deeds and glorify God on the day he visits us . . . Always be prepared to give an answer to everyone who asks you to give the reason for the hope that you have" (1 Peter 2.12; 3.15).

And both great Apostles merely took Jesus at his word: "You are the light of the world. A town built on a hill cannot be hidden. Neither do people light a lamp and put it under a bowl. Instead they put it on its stand, and it gives light to everyone in the house. In the same way, let your light shine before others, that they may see your good deeds and glorify your Father in heaven" (Matthew 5.14-16).

Let this sink in for a minute. Yesterday we emphasized that mission begins in prayer because mission is always initiated and energized by God.

---

[59] Minicius Felix, *Octavius,* 31.7; 38.6. Of course we shouldn't underestimate how much they actively and intentionally talked about their faith. More on that tomorrow.

[60] Alan Kreider, *The Change of Conversion and the Origin of Christendom* (Eugene: Wipf & Stock, 1999), 11-12.

Today Paul reminds us that from a human standpoint, our first move is not to say certain things but to walk a certain way.

In one sense the entire letter has been about this twofold nature of mission. Finally Paul makes explicit what has served as an undercurrent all along. Colossians 1.1–2.15 unpacked and celebrated the action of God in Christ that revealed and accomplished the salvation of the world. Colossians 2.16–4.1 then described the faithful human response: As individuals in community, be transformed into the image of Jesus. Become like him in every way by bringing your conscious lives in line with the Life implanted into your souls.

This is the transformation people notice: gentleness and humility replacing anger and greed; people of all races and ethnicities establishing joyful unity as one body; churches who not only worship together – no small feat in itself – but stick around long enough to transform conflicts into opportunities for forgiveness and burden-sharing; marriages marked by mutual submission and the love of Christ; parents who love their kids and children who listen to their parents; management and labor working for the same Boss and toward the same ends; grateful, attentive people who pray. These strange beauties pose questions in their minds.

And these questions present us with an opportunity – a "moment" as Paul here calls it. Paul actually uses one of two Greek words for "time." *Chronos* refers to chronological time, the kind of time we watch tick away on a clock. *Kairos*, which Paul uses here, refers less to a particular minute like 10:40 or 3:38 and more to the possibilities every such minute provides for something significant to happen. For instance, 12:46 AM on May 24, 2010 means something to me because this was the actual moment my child entered the world.

Paul says to seize the possible moments people's questions present. The word *capitalize* or "buy up" comes from the marketplace and means taking advantage of a bargain. This isn't the purchase that immediately results in buyer's remorse or the feeling that you may have just wasted hard-earned money. Quite the opposite! This is when you buy something you don't even need simply because you can't pass up the offer. This is when you get two just in case you'll never find the same item in the same size and color for the same price. This is when you beeline to the cash register because you wonder if the sale will close before you reach the end of your shopping list. This is when you don't even make it back to the car before texting all your friends, "You won't believe the deal I just found! Stop what ur doing, get here now, and bring ur plastic! :-D!!!!!"

We'll talk tomorrow about what to do with these opportune moments. For now we need to temper our excitement[61] and remember this solemn truth: Such moments – the ones when people ask questions for which the answer is Jesus, when we get to see the joy of men and women coming to know Jesus for the first time – will not happen unless our actions earn them.

---

[61] Be honest, some of you just thought about what kind of sales you'd find if you put down the book and drove immediately to whatever store or mall you love best!

Words
Chapter 38 – Colossians 4.6

Never underestimate the power of words. Sometimes we make statements that have an impact far beyond what we might expect.

After class on the first day of the second semester of my sophomore year in college, my roommate walked in and said, "Dude, I met your wife." I had no idea who she was. We've now been married almost a decade. Still might have happened had he said nothing, but who knows.

Around that same time I became fascinated with the Apostle Paul. One day a friend casually said to me, "I think maybe you're more interested in Paul than Jesus." I thought that was a silly thing to say, because my interest in Paul was rooted in my commitment to Jesus. But I took it to heart and started to focus not just on what Paul said about Jesus, but what Jesus himself said and did. I spent the next decade obsessing over learning about the real Jesus, which has borne fruit in more than one dimension. I may not have walked that path had my friend not slightly misinterpreted my appreciation for Paul, *or had he not been willing to call me on it.*

What we say to one another matters, which explains why the Bible makes such a big deal about our words. Jesus himself said, "I tell you that everyone will have to give account on the day of judgment for every empty word they have spoken. For by your words you will be acquitted, and by your words you will be condemned" (Matthew 12.36-37). His brother James was even more colorful, "All kinds of animals, birds, reptiles and sea

204

creatures are being tamed and have been tamed by mankind, but no human being can tame the tongue. It is a restless evil, full of deadly poison. With the tongue we praise our Lord and Father, and with it we curse human beings, who have been made in God's likeness. Out of the same mouth come praise and cursing. My brothers and sisters, this should not be" (James 3.7-10).

It's also why the Bible so strongly highlights talking to others about Jesus. Paul, for instance, writes in Romans 10.12-15:

> For there is no difference between Jew and Gentile —the same Lord is Lord of all and richly blesses all who call on him, for, "Everyone who calls on the name of the Lord will be saved. How, then, can people call on the one they have not believed in? And how can they believe in the one of whom they have not heard? And how can they hear without someone preaching to them? And how can anyone preach unless they are sent? As it is written: "How beautiful are the feet of those who bring good news!"

The technical term for telling others the good news about Jesus is "evangelism." Maybe you hate that word. Maybe it makes you think about a guy holding judgmental signs on a street corner, or finding church ads on your windshield in the grocery store parking lot, or someone knocking on your door and asking, "If you died tonight, where would you spend eternity?" Evangelism gets a bad rap in our world, sometimes for good reasons. But regardless of your feelings about the word, what it means is not something we can take or leave. If you are a follower of Jesus, you share the responsibility of telling others who he is and why it matters. Notice how after Paul talks about how own ministry of witnessing to Jesus, he puts the entire church on watch for similar opportunities:

> *Pray for us so that God might open to us a door for the word, so we can tell the mystery of Christ for which I have been bound, so that I might disclose it appropriately. Walk wisely toward outsiders, capitalizing on the moment. May your speech always be gracious, seasoned with salt so you'll know how you should answer each person.*   – Colossians 4.3-6

Obviously we must never forget yesterday's lesson: Our words about Jesus mean nothing unless they build on our lives. We can't rightly share Jesus without showing Jesus. But if a common problem is words without deeds, the answer is not deeds without words. The answer is actions and words together.

We *promote* the gospel with our lives and then we *pronounce* the gospel with our lips.[62] Don't worry, we're not talking about going to a baseball game, running onto the field during the national anthem, grabbing the mic and warning everyone to "turn or burn." We're talking about the many times during the normal course of our lives when we have opportunities to articulate for people what we believe about Jesus and why – in elevators, at PTA brunches, on our streets, around dinner tables, and so on.

Paul mentions two aspects of the task of pronouncing the gospel: what we say and how we say it. As far as what to say, Paul gives three focal points. First, we answer questions about our faith. Remember that Paul assumes our lives will draw people's attention. People notice when we live differently than those around us. Because we don't talk about women the same way or spend money like everyone else or respond to enemies with vengeance, people wonder. And when we have people's attention, when they notice, when they wonder, they ask: "Why do you live like that?" This question becomes an opportunity, not to cram Bible verses down people's throats but to explain why we believe and hope and love. Do you know right now what you'd say if someone asked you why?

Second, we tell the story of what God has done in our lives through Christ. Paul's story has been caught up in Christ's story, to the extent that he doesn't mind being *bound* with chains if it means more people can come to know more Jesus. It's not a bad idea to know ahead of time how you would share your story. It's not complicated either. If you need help, here's an easy three-point outline: (1) Who I was before I met Jesus. (2) How I met Jesus. (3) Who I am now because of Jesus. If you were raised in the church, just slightly adjust the first two: (1) Who I'd be without Jesus. (2) Why I made this faith my own. (3) Who I am now because of Jesus.

No life is too bad to be redeemed or too boring to make a difference. Never underestimate what God can do with your story.

---

[62] I got this idea from John Dickson's *The Best Kept Secret in Christian Mission* (Grand Rapids: Zondervan, 2010). He uses the language of promoting and proclaiming.

Third and most importantly, we tell the story of Jesus. Notice the definitive content of Paul's communication: *the word* or *mystery of Christ*. Sometimes you'll get a chance to tell the entire story: God sent Jesus from heaven to earth to re-establish God's kingdom and save us from our sins through his life, sacrificial death, and resurrection.

More often, as you're talking to friends or loved ones, you might think of a particular story from the Gospels that fits the moment. Paul specifically mentions answering *each person*, alluding to the importance of discerning what to say in each specific situation. If you're speaking to someone broken over his or her sin, maybe you explain how Jesus' death atones for sin or tell about how Jesus didn't condemn a woman caught in adultery but gently called her to a better way (John 7.53-8.11). If you have an academic friend who considers Jesus an intellectual lightweight, you might point to one of the many times Jesus stumped his opponents in debate (for example, Matthew 22.15-46). If you know someone overwhelmed by conflicts on the outside and fears within, you could share about Jesus walking on water or calming the storm (Matthew 14.22-36; Mark 4.35-31).

"Evangelism" isn't quantum physics, and it's not a sales pitch where you shoulder pressure to close the deal. You don't have to be a genius, an extrovert, or an entrepreneur. You are merely a witness. You are, as the old saying goes, one blind beggar telling other blind beggars where you found bread.

And no blind beggar poses as the smartest person in the world. Neither do we step into the role of self-appointed judge of humanity – crime dogs hunting down sin and condemning wrongdoers at every turn. Don't forget that Paul clarifies not only what we say, but also how we say it. *May your speech always be gracious*, he writes, *seasoned with salt so you'll know how you should answer each person*. We all know vegetables are good for us, but few of us enjoy them without a pinch of salt. We ought to have a sense of urgency in speaking of Jesus, but not so much that we become insensitive. Our words must be tactful, gentle, palatable, and interesting rather than needlessly offensive, harsh, irrelevant, or dull.

The world is dying to hear the message we have been given – and we've been given it precisely to enjoy and then share with others. Don't hinder what God wants to do in the lives of your family and friends by saying nothing. Speak clearly. Speak kindly. Speak Jesus.

Team
Chapter 39 – Colossians 4.7-15

Let's begin with today's text:

Tychicus will tell you all about me. He is a beloved brother, faithful servant, and fellow bondslave in the Lord, and I sent him to you for this very reason, that you might know what's going on in my life and that your hearts might be encouraged. I sent him with Onesimus the beloved brother, who is one of your own. They'll tell you everything happening here. Aristarchus my fellow prisoner greets you. Also, if Mark (Barnabas's cousin, about whom you received a command) comes to you then welcome him, and also Jesus who is called Justus. Among my coworkers for the kingdom of God only these are Jewish, and they became a comfort to me.

Epaphras greets you, and he too is one of your own, a servant of Christ Jesus, always striving in the prayers on your behalf, so that you might stand mature and completely full in all God's will. I testify for him that he has great concern for you, as well as those in Laodicea and Hierapolis. Luke the beloved doctor greets you, and Demas too. Greet the brothers and sisters in Laodicea, and Nympha and those in the church that gathers in her house.

– Colossians 4.7-15

We believe that every word of the Bible is inspired by God, but do you ever wonder why God inspired such seemingly pointless details? Who are these people and why did they make it into sacred Scripture? Believe it or not, I think this passage presents us with four principles so important that if we ignore them, we will miss out on God's ideal plan for our lives.

(1) God calls us to work in teams. What God is calling us to do, we cannot do alone. We spent all last week talking about all the relationships that make up the community of faith, as well as the practices that sustain our life together. Here we see that Paul lives what he preaches about community. In these short verses he mentions no less than ten coworkers! Without these people he simply wouldn't be the Apostle Paul we know today. They helped him clarify his thinking, keep the faith through nearly unbearable hardships, plant churches, send letters, and no doubt much more.

Paul learned this lesson by experience. After Paul met Jesus he immediately went around telling others what he now knew: Jesus is Israel's Messiah and the world's true Lord. A few years into this work, he went to Jerusalem so he could connect with the official apostles who were leading the church. The only problem was that no one in Jerusalem trusted him. They actually feared he was a double agent, only posing as a Jesus-follower so he could find out who was on the inside and then turn them in later on. Paul was stuck.

But then Barnabas came along. Barnabas was nicknamed "the Encourager" thanks to his habit of finding struggling people, putting his arm around them, and walking with them to places they could never reach on their own. Barnabas vouched for Paul and because everyone trusted Barnabas, they gave Paul a shot. The rest is literally history, and this history continued to be marked by community. This point is simple: God always calls us to work in teams.

(2) God's teams are diverse. If everyone in your church (or on your team) looks like you and dresses like you and shares the same socio-economic status or education level, that's a little weird. Not necessarily bad, but probably not good either. At the very least, we can say quite clearly that at this stage of Paul's career, he surrounded himself with all different sorts of people. For starters, here we see both men and women. Secondly, we've got both Jews (as Paul specifically mentions) and Gentiles. Interestingly enough, even though Paul is Jewish, the majority of his coworkers are Gentile. We see folks from completely opposite sides of the social spectrum as well. We

have a slave (Onesimus) as well as a woman who, as a household manager, most likely owned slaves of her own (Nympha). We also have a doctor in Luke, who was also not too shabby a historian and author in his own right. (This is the same Luke who wrote the Gospel of Luke and the book of Acts.) All sorts of divisions – ethnic, cultural, gender, socio-economic – are transcended in Paul's band of mighty men and women.

(3) *Conflict will happen.* This shouldn't come as a surprise given our diversity, as well as the general human tendency not to get along forever. Two conflicts are represented in Paul's travel updates. First and sadly, the Demas Paul mentions here will later love the world too much to see the mission through (see 2 Timothy 4.10). The second explains Paul's mention of Mark. Many years previously, Paul and Barnabas had taken young Mark with them on a missionary journey, only to see Mark desert them and head home early. Some time later Barnabas wanted to bring Mark along a second time (Barnabas and Mark were cousins), but Paul refused. The dispute was so serious that Paul and Barnabas decided to go their separate ways! (You can read about this in Acts 15.36-41.) But by this later point in Paul's life, you can see that Mark has been fully reinstated in his heart and his plans. We should expect conflict, but whenever possible we shouldn't let division have the last word.

(4) *Don't count anybody out.* This point flows out of both the last two. Note once more the lesson of Mark: those who quit on us one day may become important allies down the road. If you have failed, don't let your past failure stop you from giving it another go. If you've been failed, don't assume that person will never come through in the future. We could again mention the unlikely pair of Onesimus and Nympha. Not only is Onesimus a slave, he is the *runaway* slave Paul writes about in Philemon. And Nympha didn't let the fact that she was a woman – and quite possibly a widow – stop her from using her resources to serve the church. We also can't forget about Epaphras. As we mentioned much earlier, his name was short for "Epaphroditus," which means he was named for Aphrodite, the famous pagan goddess of love. We don't want to over-speculate, but we can guess that he didn't spend his growing up years faithfully worshiping God.

Who you were does not define who you are. And who you are today doesn't dictate who you will become tomorrow. As Martin Luther put it, God can draw straight lines with crooked sticks. He can work through the person you can't stand. And he can also work through you.

So the next time you go to church or Sunday school or a small group meeting, look around. These people are your teammates – no matter how different, annoying, or hopeless they may seem. Thankfully, your responsibility isn't to like everything about them. But writing them off is not an option for you.

The goal lies somewhere between trying to be best friends and having nothing to do with each other. We are teammates, we need each other, and God can do through us together more than he can with any of us on our own. In the end we must learn to ask two questions about each other. We start with this: What is God doing in you and how can I help? At the very least we'll get the same answer Epaphras did: Pray. He prayed for his fellow Jesus-followers that they might reach full maturity in doing God's will. And as we pray, no doubt God will lay on our heart all sorts of possible next steps. Many times the answer will lead to another level: What does God want to do through us *together*?

In an old Peanuts cartoon, Lucy demanded that her brother Linus change TV channels and then threatened him with her fist if he didn't.

"What makes you think you can walk right in here and take over?" asked Linus.

"These five fingers," said Lucy. "Individually they are nothing, but when I curl them together like this into a single unit, they form a weapon that is terrible to behold."

"What channel do you want?" sighed Linus.

Turning away, Linus looked at his fingers and said, "Why can't you guys work together like that?"

When you get frustrated with all those imperfect people in your church – to the point that you think you might be better off on your own – remember the principle of fingers and fists: God can accomplish more through five of us working together than hundreds of us on our own.

Fuel

Chapter 40 – Colossians 4.16

Isn't it interesting that Paul wrote letters we'll never get to read? Paul probably wrote dozens we don't have, and one we know of for sure. In today's text, Paul specifically mentions a letter lost to history.

> *And whenever you read this letter, see to it that it is also read in the Laodicean church, and you also read the one from Laodicea.*
>
> – Colossians 4.16

What is this letter from the Laodicean church? Scholars have offered different proposals through the years. Some have said that it's a letter from the Laodicean church to the Colossians. This theory never gained much ground because it doesn't fit the grammar Paul uses or the letter-sharing he seems to be talking about. Others have suggested Philemon as a possibility. But Philemon lived in Colossae, so that can't be right. Still others have suggested that Paul refers to the letter we know as Ephesians, which is a possibility. Many early manuscripts of Ephesians are missing the phrase "in Ephesus" from the opening lines, indicating that this letter was meant to be circulated through many churches. (And Ephesus, Colossae, and Laodicea are all in the same general vicinity.) Nonetheless early traditions place Ephesians in Ephesus, and the most likely explanation is that Paul's letter to Laodicea has indeed been lost.

But the most interesting thing about this letter isn't the fact that we'll never read it. It's the fact that the Christians in Colossae did. What I mean is that it wasn't written to them, yet Paul specifically tells them to obtain and read it as if it were.

Have you ever noticed that when we read the New Testament, about half of the time we're reading someone else's mail? These are personal letters from apostles to churches (and in some cases, even to individuals), and yet we read them as if written to us. Why?

Well, because they were written to us. And Paul's brief comment helps explain why. From the very beginning, everyone in the church acknowledged that when an official apostle wrote an official letter, there was something special about it. And this something special made their writings relevant to all Jesus-followers everywhere. They wouldn't finalize the Bible as we know it for a couple hundred years, but here we see evidence that the process began as quickly as these now-biblical books were written.

This process of "canonization" built on the recognition that God has specially identified certain writings to have lasting authority and significance for his church.[63] We believe that when we hold the Bible, we're holding the inspired and therefore authoritative word of God.

But what good is an inspired book if all we do is hold it?

One time a young man was making plans to study theology in college when his father expressed disapproval over the school he had chosen.

"That place is full of liberals!" he scolded. "By the time they get through with you, you won't even believe the Bible anymore."

But he went anyway. The school was far away and clearly the boy and his father weren't best friends, so a couple years went by before he returned home for a break between semesters. His father wasted no time putting junior to the test.

"So," his father inquired, "was I right? You probably think the Bible is a bunch of fairy tales. How about Jonah? You probably deny that the Jonah story actually happened, don't you?"

"You're right dad, I don't think Jonah actually spent three days in the belly of a big fish, though I do think the story teaches an important lesson."

---

[63] The word canon simply means "standard," and canonization refers to the process by which the church recognized and determined which books met the standards for belonging in the Bible.

"I told you those liberals would ruin you!"

"Tell you what, dad," the son replied, "How about you and I read the story together, and you can explain to me why you think we have to read it literally?"

Never one to back down from a challenge, his dad happily obliged. He grabbed his Bible off the shelf and quickly thumbed its pages in search of Jonah. A few minutes went by and he got a little agitated because he couldn't find it.

"Hold on, son, I know where it is. It has always been one of my favorites."

After a while he gave up and turned to the Table of Contents. He then flipped to the correct page number and was astonished when once again, Jonah was not there. He looked closer and noticed why.

"What in the world? Someone tore pages out of my Bible!"

"Yes, dad, I did. Two years ago. Clearly you didn't notice. So let me ask you a question: What is the difference between me 'denying' the Bible and you ignoring it?"[64]

God didn't inspire the Bible so we could admire it. He gave us the Bible so we would read it.

When God gave messages to his prophets, he would occasionally tell them to eat the words he has spoken. Not figuratively, mind you. He told them to literally put the scroll in their mouths, chew, and swallow. Ezekiel testifies that he did so and "it tasted as sweet as honey in my mouth" (Ezekiel 3.3). Often in the Psalms we are told to "meditate" on the Scriptures. Like a cow slowly and repeatedly chewing her cud, we slow down, concentrate, and review the words in our mind again and again. Never forget that God didn't give us the Bible so we could admire or defend it. He inspired Scripture so we would read it.

I hope you have a high view of Scripture, but just as importantly, I hope you have a habit of actually digesting what it says.

I know the Bible is a big, strange, confusing, frustrating book. I'm sure you've tried to read it a dozen times, but once you got to Leviticus you gave up. I can't solve all your problems in a few paragraphs and I wouldn't want

---

[64] I haven't been able to track down the original source for this story, but I first heard it from Jim Johnson, Lead Minister at Sunnybrook Christian Church in Stillwater, OK.

to even if I could, but here are a few general guidelines to help get you started.[65]

(1) Read the Bible with the right attitude. Simply put, read with a readiness to obey. Read with an open heart and mind in search of God and truth and transformation. Don't read to get smart and prove someone else wrong. Don't read to prove God wrong. Don't read to check one more item off your spiritual to-do list. Always remember, "The goal is not for us to get through the Scriptures. The goal is to get the Scriptures through us."[66] Read with a humble desire to hear from God and a willingness to follow wherever he leads.

(2) Interpret the Bible responsibly. Entire books have been written on what this means, but here are a few quick things to remember. First, when you're reading specific verses or chapters, keep the big picture in mind. Scripture tells one continuous story, and its various parts are significant for us in different ways. Know where you are in the story. Second, never forget that the biblical story centers on Jesus. He is our grid for faithfully interpreting every word. Always read with one eye glued to Christ. Third, notice the details. If I can say this without it sounding cheesy, read the Bible like a love letter. Look at the individual words, and notice how they fit together to create meaning. If the Bible uses an image for God, actually picture that image in your imagination and explore what you can learn from it. If you find the same word repeated over and over, ask why. Finally, always pay attention to context. You don't like your words being taken out of context. God doesn't either. God didn't give us a bunch of individual verses, but whole books that flow together like a good argument or an alluring song. Interpret words and verses and paragraphs in light of the words and verses and paragraphs on either side of them.

(3) Read the Bible in community. Paul took this for granted, because his churches probably only had one copy of the letters you and I carry with us wherever we go. While I'm endlessly grateful for those who gave their lives so we could each have our own Bible, reading together should still be the normal way of encountering Scripture. Sometimes this means literally opening Scripture in one another's presence, reading aloud, and discussing. Other times it might mean a few friends follow the same reading plan and

---

[65] If you need a practical tool to get started and follow a scheduled routine, check out the Life Journal and www.lifejournal.cc.

[66] John Ortberg, *The Life You've Always Wanted* (Grand Rapids: Zondervan, 1997), 184.

share their thoughts over email. At the very least we read not only to hear a word for ourselves but also to find new ways to encourage others with the truth.

At the end of the day, just read the Bible. Reading the Bible doesn't necessarily mean you are a good Jesus-follower. But it's virtually impossible to become a good Jesus-follower without reading the Bible. Reading the Bible is like fuel. Having gas in the tank doesn't mean your car is going somewhere. But you'll have a hard time getting anywhere without it.

Lines
Chapter 41 – Colossians 4.17

If I were a betting man, I would drop good money on the fact that you have never thought twice about Archippus. Why would you? He isn't exactly on anyone's list of Bible heroes or patron saints. Yet he is mentioned by name in the only two documents written to his hometown of Colossae (Philemon and Colossians). And both times he gets more than a passing glance. In Philemon, Paul dignifies him with the title of "our fellow soldier," no small compliment from the great Apostle himself. But here in Colossians he kind of gets called out: *And tell Archippus, "See to the ministry you received in the Lord, that you fulfill it"* (Colossians 4.17).

"Called out" might be a bit strong. It's hard to know if Archippus was shirking his responsibility or was simply in the process of completing whatever task he received. Matter of fact, it's hard to know much of anything about Archippus and the ministry he *received in the Lord*. All we know is that he was called to serve in some way. That's the idea behind the word *ministry*. It was used for everything from waiting tables to making big decisions about the church's direction.

We have no idea what his task was, and I'm kind of glad about that. Why? Because if we knew, we'd be even less likely to pay attention. If we knew Archippus was merely told to take care of a particular widow or fill the communion trays, we'd probably lose interest. If, on the other hand, we knew he was given some daunting task, we'd use that as an excuse to label ourselves insufficient. At least as it is, we're curious. But more valuable than stoking our curiosity is the reminder that each of us has been given responsibilities that we need to fulfill.

Some of us have a tendency to see what everyone else should do or can do. "You know she just comes to church, sings, listens, and goes home. The least she could do is serve in the nursery or help out in the office during the week." "Man, that guy is gifted. Words flow out of his mouth like verbal silk. And he seems to genuinely like people too. If I was that fluent or kind, I'd be doing great things too." In these and other ways we become so focused on their responsibilities that we ignore or minimize our own. Even the Apostle Peter, when Jesus was talking to him about his future, pointed to the Apostle John and said, "What about him?" I love Jesus' response: "If I want him to remain alive until I return, what is that to you? You must follow me" (John 21.22).

What you need to realize is that only you can do what you can do. No one else can accomplish precisely what you can accomplish to move God's mission forward. Think about that for a second, because when you first hear it you'll either miss what I'm saying or automatically assume it can't be true. But it is true. Only you can do precisely what you can do to make an impact in the name of Jesus. No one else has your same combination of body, face, personality, voice, gifts, skills, competencies, job, friendships, street address, and schedule. God can fill many holes with other people, but if you don't do your part then some opportunities will be missed. Some good will go undone. Some lines will forever remain unsaid.

Often we find ourselves asking, "What is God's will for my life?" Or less formally, "God, what do you want me to do?" Throughout the years, wise teachers have broken this question into two categories: God's specific will and God's general will. God's specific will refers to specific things he wants us to do. For instance, Paul was called to the specific task of telling Gentiles that Jesus is Messiah and Lord. Similarly, Peter was commissioned to continue working with Jews toward the same end. We talk today about God "calling" certain people to move overseas, work for a church, have kids, or start a business that benefits the world. Whatever "ministry" Archippus received may fall into this category. God's specific will for your life looks different from his specific will for my life.

God's general will, as you might have guessed, refers to what God desires for all of us. For example, Paul says in another place, "Rejoice always, pray continually, give thanks in all circumstances; for this is God's will for you in Christ Jesus" (1 Thessalonians 5.16-18). God doesn't just want this for specific people; God wants this for all of us. In this category we could include any number of things we've learned right here in Colossians. God's general will includes us growing in our knowledge of God, bearing fruit in all kinds of good works, developing the kind of virtues that characterize God's new creation, and so on.

To be honest, we often make "finding God's will" more complicated than it is. Sometimes I think we emphasize God's specific will because we don't like what we know of God's general will. (Mark Twain once remarked that it wasn't the parts of the Bible he didn't understand that bothered him, but the parts he did.[67]) The Bible places much more emphasis on God's general will, which is right there for all of us to see. Focus your energies on becoming the person God wants you to be, and very likely the specific tasks will be taken care of.

If you're wrestling with this question and want a little more guidance, here is one more thought. Look around you and identify as many needs as you can – in your neighborhood, at your church. Then prayerfully ask questions of your list. Which of these am I capable of? Which would I find joy in accomplishing? Which will no one else do if I don't? Which are the greatest needs right now? And eventually just decide to take on an item from your list. Even if it isn't the perfect place for you to be serving, chances are God will redirect you as you go. It's always easier to steer a moving vehicle than a parked car. Start doing something. Start serving somewhere. And trust God and the church to move you where the mission needs you most.

A young man came to his parents and asked to take a yearlong class in public speaking and theater. Their first thought was, "You already talk too much as it is!" But they said no problem and to go for it. He attended diligently week after week for an entire year, and at the end of the year they had a show. There were speeches and plays and dramatic readings. This young man was in one of the plays. He was a king, and he did look pretty regal – until the queen walked out and was about a foot taller, casting a shadow on his glory! He had only three lines in the whole production, and they were the last words of the closing scene of the final act of the very last

---

[67] *The Wit and Wisdom of Mark Twain*, edited by Alex Ayres (New York: HarperCollins, 1987), 23.

play. Anyway you looked at it, he was not the star. But you'd never know that by looking at his parents, who were beaming.

Afterwards someone approached his father and asked, "What did you think of your boy?"

And his father said, "I think he said his lines. He was prepared. He was ready. He said his lines and he said them well. Not too soon, not too late; not too loud, not too soft; but just right, he said his lines."[68]

Thousands upon thousands of people throughout the centuries have read *this* story, taken their place in it just like Archippus, and said their lines. They've built hospitals and brought down dictators and planted churches; they've changed diapers and greeted visitors and told Bible stories to kids; they've prayed for the lost and encouraged the depressed and sat with the dying; they've raised children and fed the hungry and taken care of widows and orphans. In these ways and so many more, they said their lines.

You are not the star of God's story. But when the curtain falls and the drama ends, who cares what the credits remember or the critics say? We play our part so we can hear one thing from our Heavenly Father: "You said your lines."

If Archippus teaches us anything, it is this: Say your lines. Not Paul's lines. Not your pastor's lines. Not my lines. Not your spouse's lines or your parents' lines or your friends' lines. Say your lines, and say them well.

You are not the lead actor. You are not the star. Jesus is. But you are not unimportant to the story. He has given you an integral role that only you can perfectly play, so for the sake of Christ and the moving forward of God's mission, say your lines.

---

[68] Bob Benson, *Laughter in the Walls* (Nashville: Generoux Nelson, 1969, 1990), 15.

Chains
Chapter 42 – Colossians 4.18

Remember my chains.

What an odd way to end a letter.

It has become something of a sport in our day to add uplifting, clever, or snarky sayings to our email signatures.

"Make it a great day."

"Be the change you want to see in the world."

"Smile, God loves you."

"My karma ran over your dogma."

"Don't wait until it's too late to start caring about what you're putting into your body."

Or my personal favorite, "Please consider the environment before printing this email." I once knew a guy who replied, "Please consider my nerves before you send me another one!"

But never in a million emails have I seen the tagline, "Remember my chains." It's so dark, so gloomy, so depressing.

Yet this is how Paul brings Colossians to a close. Paul ends with a reminder that he's not writing from a palace. He's writing from a prison cell. With a reminder that Jesus might get you beat up and in trouble with the law. With a reminder that pursuing more Jesus often means receiving less comfort. With a reminder that the gospel is explosive and you handle it at your own risk. With a reminder that this stuff might get you killed.

There are two directions we can profitably take Paul's parting shot. First, we can remember those who are currently in chains for the gospel. We call to mind and pray for those who are being harassed, beaten, and even killed for refusing to let go of Jesus. Persecution is hardly a thing of the past. I think about the story of Phum, a 17-year-old Laotian girl who recently became a follower of Jesus. When her family learned of her conversion, they forbade her going to church. She persisted, but her father often gave her extra chores on Sunday so she couldn't attend. Other times he would sign up the family to work far away from home on Sundays so she had no choice but to miss. When they stayed local and she finished her chores, her older brother would stand at the door and beat her with a wooden stick when she tried to walk by. The same brother has since burned her Bible and hymnbook. She continues to follow Jesus as best she can, but, well, it isn't easy.[69]

Phum's story is hardly an isolated incident. Twenty-two churches have already been forced to close in Indonesia this year alone. Just a few weeks ago, a man in Nigeria strapped a bomb to his body, drove his car into a Christian church, and exploded – killing two and injuring dozens. We're actually coming out of the bloodiest century ever for followers of Jesus. During the past decade, over 100,000 Christians have been killed for their faith every year. That's almost three hundred martyrs every day, twelve per hour, or one every five minutes.

That is a lot of people who, like Paul, will choose to die rather than deny Jesus. Apparently they've found in Jesus something worth pursuing at all costs. Literally. Martyrs make us stop and think. What would I do if I was being treated like a baseball or staring down the barrel of a gun? Could I keep the faith that far? Is Jesus really worth that much?

Second, we can reflect upon our own death. Paul's references to "chains" cluster around the last few letters of his life. Paul sensed the end was near. He knew he would soon die, and death has a way of centering people.

I have a friend who commissioned the building of his own casket when he was thirty-five. If that isn't enough, he later put it in his office. To this day, when I go visit him, I sit in the guest chair with my friend to my left

---

[69] Similar stories are frequently told, along with other info, on the Voice Of the Martyrs website. http://www.persecution.com/public/newsroom.aspx?story_ID=NTEw. Accessed 6/14/12.

and his casket to my right. If you ask him why, he'll just say he doesn't want to forget the one thing he knows will eventually happen to him: he will die.

I will too. So will you.

We can either ignore this fact or let it appropriately shape the way we spend the remainder of our days.

My friend's in-office casket wouldn't seem strange to many spiritual masters through the centuries. Wise Jesus-followers have often singled out contemplating our own eventual demise as one of the most beneficial spiritual disciplines we can practice. Throughout church history, many of our best teachers have advised that we regularly contemplate our death.

In his fifteenth century masterpiece *The Imitation of Christ*, Thomas a Kempis pulls no punches: "A short time is all you have here . . . Your every thought and action should be that of a man who is to die this day." Or again, "Blessed is he who has the hour of death always before his eyes and daily prepares for it." Or more specifically, "When you rise in the morning, think that you will not see evening; and when evening comes, do not be too certain that you will rise in the morning. *Be always ready*, therefore, and so live that death may not find you unprepared." Later he puts it as simple as possible: "Always think of death!"[70]

Many medieval monks actually kept skulls in their rooms with the Latin phrase *Summus Moribundus* etched into them, which means, "We are destined to die."

Centuries later in *An Introduction to the Devout Life*, Francis de Sales gave the following three-step guide to structuring your quiet time with the Lord: "(1) Place yourself in the Presence of God. (2) Ask His Grace. (3) Suppose yourself to be on your deathbed, in the last extremity, without the smallest hope of recovery."[71] Not exactly positive thinking, but then again positive thinking sometimes doesn't align well with reality.

You are going to die. And the fact that you are going to die should make you think twice about how you live. To what or whom have you given yourself? What do you believe in? Who are you working for? What are you pursuing? What you are seeking *more* of? Do you want more laughs? More thrills? More friends? More sex? More toys? More curves? More knowledge? More accolades? More security?

---

[70] Thomas a Kempis, *The Imitation of Christ* (New York: Random House, 1998), 33-35.
[71] Francis de Sales, *An Introduction to the Devout Life* (New York, Random House, 2002), 25.

You have a limited amount of life to fill. What are you going to fill it with? And why?

People at the edge of life tend to see things clearly. Paul did. And the question for him wasn't so much "What can I take with me?" but "To whom am I going?"

Paul has not hidden his agenda from us. He believes with every breath in the all-sufficiency of Jesus Christ, and he wants us to believe the same.

He began Colossians by reminding us what we already know, have, and look forward to in Christ. Here we have received a call to be different, an invitation rooted in the hope of the gospel – a gospel that just so happens to be true and active in bearing fruit all over the world. Here we have been given not only hope for the next life but a glorious future in the meantime as we experience more of the salvation found only in the name of Jesus.

He then overwhelmed our senses with a mind-blowing depiction of this Jesus, who alone perfectly displays both the identity of God and the meaning of humanity. Nothing exists that didn't come through him, wasn't made for him, and isn't held together this very moment by him. Not even the most powerful entities in our world – neither visible nor invisible – can claim autonomy from or power over him, for he is Lord. Paul clarified that this Jesus isn't all talk either, but rather has invaded our broken sphere of reality with new life from above – the power of forgiveness, reconciliation, peace. Everything in both creation and redemption will always remain rooted in him.

Of this we can be confident, Paul explained, for here in Jesus the millennia-long mission of God finds resolution. Here in Jesus we see the delicacy that reveals our plate of leftovers for what it is. Here we see the fullness of Deity with a human heart and mind and skin. Into this story we have been written, so that our story, too, is resolved by being redeemed. Because of him our Accuser has no case. Because of him the Intimidators have lost their powers of intimidation.

In him we grow with the growth that comes from God. This growth doesn't center on regulations or flights of spiritual fancy, but on the indwelling Christ who implants in us the life of new creation. This life takes hold of us, shakes us out of our death-complacency, and renews us after our original design. Our old identities shrink as our imagination is enlarged by his dream for us – the dream of a transformed community of love and grace, a community that stays together and even sings together, a community whose worship extends beyond Sunday morning to encompass every word, every deed, and every relationship in our lives.

And in him we go because by him we have been sent on mission to savor and spread this gospel that won't let us leave. For this task we have been adequately resourced with one another and the enduring power of God's Word, so that each of us may faithfully fulfill our part – no matter the cost or temporary consequence. Death does not scare us, not because we want to die but because we know who awaits us when we do.

Throughout this journey Paul has relentlessly reminded us that we don't need more than Christ. All we need is more of what we already have. All we need is more Jesus.

Sources

I didn't want to merely drift into my fourth decade. I knew I wanted something to center myself on Christ, so I read Colossians and underlined every reference to Jesus, whether by name or pronoun. I'd never realized just how Christ-centered this letter was, so I dusted off my Greek translation tools, ordered a few commentaries, asked some friends if I could stay in their coastal condo, and went for it. A couple months later our lead pastor and I met to discuss possible future book projects. We'd had fun with *Jesus in 3D* and were ready to tackle something new. Turns out Colossians was a perfect fit for what both of us were thinking, and thus *moreJESUS* was born.

We both decided that what our churches needed was not another academic work or commentary, but more of an exegetically grounded series of devotional meditations. Nevertheless I want to credit all those authors and books that were instrumental in shaping my understanding of Colossians. For my first round of study I took the Colossians commentaries by Andrew Lincoln, Peter T. O'Brien, Ben Witherington, and N. T. Wright (Tyndale). I also benefited from Leonard Sweet and Frank Viola's *Jesus Manifesto* and *Colossians Remixed* by Brian Walsh and Sylvia Keesmaat. Because I began this first round of study without a book in mind, I may have incorporated some of their thoughts into my own. My apologies for any places I've not been able to decipher and cite appropriately.

After deciding to write a book, I went through another round of study with the commentaries from G. B. Caird, James Dunn, Murray Harris, Margaret MacDonald, Douglas Moo, Jerry Sumney, Charles Talbert, and Marriane Meye Thompson. I also learned much from specific studies on Colossians including *Christ the All-Sufficient One* by William Barclay, *Greed As Idolatry* by Brian Rosner, and *In Christ, In Colossae* by Derek Tidball, as well as the following New Testament Introductions: *Introducing the New Testament* by Paul Achtemeier, Joel Green, & Marianne Meye Thompson, *An Introduction to the New Testament* by David de Silva, *Apostle of the Crucified Lord* by Michael Gorman, and *Writings of the New Testament* by Luke Timothy Johnson.

For historical background information I also relied on *Documents and Images for the Study of Paul* edited by Neil Elliott and Mark Reasoner, *Backgrounds of Early Christianity* by Everett Ferguson, *The Roman World 44 BC – AD 180* by Martin Goodman, Part 1 of *Paul and Empire* edited by Richard Horsley, and *The Greco-Roman World* by James Jeffers. Also helpful in various ways were *The Triumph of God* by J. Christian Beker, *Christ the Center* by Dietrich Bonhoeffer, *Christ and Creation* by Colin Gunton, *Naming the Powers* by Walter Wink, and *The Climax of the Covenant* and *Following Jesus* by N. T. Wright, as well as everything cited in the footnotes.

CPSIA information can be obtained
at www.ICGtesting.com
Printed in the USA
LVOW01*2257100217
523657LV00005B/7/P